Patterns
of
Juvenile
Delinquency

LAW AND CRIMINAL JUSTICE SERIES

Series Editor: James A. Inciardi

Division of Criminal Justice, University of Delaware

The **Law and Criminal Justice Series** provides students in criminal justice, criminology, law, sociology, and related fields with a set of short textbooks on major topics and subareas of the field. The texts range from books that introduce the basic elements of criminal justice for lower division under- graduates to more advanced topics of current interest for advanced under- graduates and beginning graduate students. Each text is concise, didactic, and produced in an inexpensive paperback as well as hardcover format. Each author addresses the major issues and areas of current concern in that topic area, reporting on and synthesizing major research done on the subject. Case examples, chapter summaries, and discussion questions are generally included in each volume to aid in classroom use. The modular format of the series provides attractive alternatives to large, expensive classroom textbooks or timely supplements to more traditional class materials.

Volumes in this series:

1: THE AMERICAN SYSTEM OF CRIMINAL JUSTICE,
  Geoffrey P. Alpert

2: PATTERNS OF JUVENILE DELINQUENCY,
  Howard B. Kaplan

3: THE IDEA OF POLICE, Carl Klockars

Additional volumes currently in development.

Patterns of Juvenile Delinquency

HOWARD B. KAPLAN

Volume 2.
Law and Criminal Justice Series

 SAGE PUBLICATIONS Beverly Hills London New Delhi

*This book is dedicated with love
to my wife, Diane Susan, and
to my children, Samuel Charles and Rachel Esther.*

For information address:

SAGE Publications, Inc.
275 South Beverly Drive
Beverly Hills, California 90212

SAGE Publications India Pvt. Ltd.   SAGE Publications Ltd
C-236 Defence Colony   28 Banner Street
New Delhi 110 024, India   London EC1Y 8QE, England

Printed in the United States of America

Library of Congress Cataloging in Publication Data

Kaplan, Howard B.
  Patterns of juvenile delinquency.

  (Law and criminal justice series ; v. 2)
  Includes index.
  1. Juvenile delinquency. I. Title. II. Series:
Law and criminal justice series ; v. 2.
HV9069.K33   1984   364.3'6   84-18015
ISBN 0-8039-2208-6
ISBN 0-8039-2209-4 (pbk.)

FIRST PRINTING

CONTENTS

ACKNOWLEDGMENTS

The research for this book was facilitated by research grant DA 02497 from the National Institute on Drug Abuse and by a research grant from the Hogg Foundation for Mental Health. My thanks to Pamela K. Derrick for her stick-to-itiveness at the word processor in the face of the tedium of the task. Special thanks to my colleague Steven S. Martin for his "above and beyond the call of duty" interest in the manuscript, for his valuable suggestions, and for his aid in the production of the drafts during the hectic days of trying to meet the publisher's deadline.

Since not all *motives* to perform delinquent acts result in delinquent behavior, Chapter 5 considers the social processes that hinder or facilitate the acting out of deviant dispositions. Motives that may counteract deviant dispositions (such as emotional commitment to conventional standards or fear of social rejection) and opportunities to learn and perform delinquent behaviors are considered among the influences upon the acting out of delinquent dispositions. Once youths have performed delinquent acts, however, the continuity of delinquent behavior is problematic. Whether or not the youth continues to perform delinquent acts will depend on the consequences of the initial performance and normally occurring maturational sequences. The processes that influence continuity or change in level or delinquent involvement are considered in Chapter 6.

In Chapter 7, the consequences of juvenile delinquency both with regard to the social responses that arise to contain such behavior and the unanticipated functions of such behavior are considered.

The foregoing chapters present a sample that I believe is representative of the theoretical orientations and empirical findings that social scientists have offered in trying to understand the origins and consequences of juvenile delinquency. In Chapter 8, by way of summarizing this material, I offer a general model of the social antecedents and consequences of juvenile delinquency. The model reflects my own synthesis of the social science literature on the subject. It is a tentative formulation that is intended to serve only as an introductory framework for the organization and evaluation of present and future theoretical statements and research findings relating to the social basis of the onset and continuity of delinquent patterns and the consequences of such patterns for the social system.

—Howard B. Kaplan
Houston, Texas

1

THE STUDY OF
JUVENILE DELINQUENCY

The proper study of the social antecedents and consequences of juvenile delinquency requires first, that we have a common understanding of the term "juvenile delinquency"; second, that we understand and evaluate the sources of the observations or data upon which we draw in order to make generalizations about the social antecedents and consequences of juvenile delinquency; and third, that we make explicit the processes by which we draw generalizations about the social antecedents and consequences of juvenile delinquency.

JUVENILE DELINQUENCY DEFINED

The study of juvenile delinquency will be made easier if three elements of the definition are clarified. Juvenile delinquency refers to any of a number of (1) behaviors (2) performed by young people (3) that are violations of laws applicable to young people's behavior.

Behavior

The definition specifies that juvenile delinquency refers to a subclass of behaviors (those performed by juveniles that are in violation of the legal norms of society). Among the behaviors that fall within the subcategory are personal assault, vandalism, and theft. This specification is an important one from the point of view of explaining the onset, continuity, and consequences of juvenile delinquency for three reasons.

First, since we are dealing with a subclass of behaviors, we are directed to explain these behaviors in the same general way that we explain other behaviors. If we wanted to explain why people behave in a certain way, then we might talk about motivation to conform to or deviate from group standards, about learning ways to adapt to situational demands, or about the opportunities for and limitations upon such behavior that are provided by the social and physical environment.

Second, since we are directed to explain behaviors, in effect we are instructed to differentiate between the behaviors and phenomena that are often confused with the behavior. These phenomena are to be explained in ways that differ from those that are appropriate for explaining the behavior. Behavior is frequently confused with the *evaluation* of the behavior in social science research. However, the explanation for the evaluation of specified behaviors may be in different terms than those appropriate for explaining the occurrence of the behavior itself. If we wanted to explain why people or groups have certain attitudes toward the behavior, we might need to consider such factors as the heterogeneity of values in a society, the conflict between groups that endorse different values, the differential power possessed by the various groups that permit the enforcement of one rather than another set of standards, and social change processes that lead to the displacement of one set of standards by another.

Third, by permitting the clear differentiation between related constructs, the specification that juvenile delinquency is behavior enhances our ability to explain the behavior in terms of the related construct and to explain the related construct (evaluation of the behavior) in terms of the behavior itself. Part of the explanation of why people behave or do not behave in certain ways concerns the expressions of social attitudes toward those behaviors. The explanations of why people express certain social attitudes, then, indirectly explain (in part) the behaviors. Conversely, part of the explanation of social attitudes toward behaviors is the *prevalence of behaviors* (the more people do something, the more acceptable the behavior becomes). Hence, the explanation of the patterns of behavior contributes indirectly to the explanation of the nature of social attitudes toward the behavior.

When considering the explanation of the social origins and consequences of juvenile delinquency in particular, a parallel distinction must be drawn between the behavior that is labelled as juvenile delinquency and the process of labeling juvenile delinquency. Again, the direct influences upon one may be quite different than the direct influences upon the other. The direct explanations of the *behavior* might be in terms of the person's needs to conform to the expectations of his membership groups or to behave in ways that reject the validity of those expectations or in such terms as fear of punishment and the opportunities to perform the behaviors. On the other hand, the direct explanations of the expression of the *social evaluation* of the behaviors as juvenile delinquency might be in terms of the differential political power of groups that endorse divergent value systems or in terms of the process of social change whereby the locus of political power and evaluative standards change. Once again, however, the direct influences upon the *performances* of the behaviors that conventional society defines as delinquent are different from the direct influences upon the process whereby particular behaviors are *evaluated* as delinquent. Since the performance of delinquent behaviors and the social evaluation of the behaviors influence each other, the determinants of the one will influence indirectly the determinants of the other. The processes influencing the social definition of certain behaviors as delinquent will be considered in Chapter 2. The mutual influences of the social definition of behavior as delinquent and the delinquent behavior itself will be considered at various points throughout the remainder of the book.

Age-Related Deviance

The definition of juvenile delinquency specifies that only violations of legal rules that are applicable to youths may be classified as part of that subcategory of behaviors. Legal rules do not necessarily apply uniformly to all segments of the population although certain behaviors may apply to all members of the society. Members of a society whether young or adult violate the law when they steal from or assault other members of a society. However, other behaviors may be forbidden solely to people who have not yet reached adult status. Juveniles violate the normative expectations of society when they purchase and consume alcoholic beverages, leave their parental home without permission, do not attend school, engage in certain patterns of sexual behavior, or consistently disobey their parents or legal guardians. Adults who engage in like activities are not regarded necessarily as in violation of formal social rules.

In short this book addresses questions relating to the social antecedents and consequences of illicit acts that are performed by youths. It ignores the question of whether or not similar acts would be illegal if performed by adults as well as questions relating to the social antecedents and consequences of illicit adult activity (which may or may not be similar to those of illicit youth activity).

Legal Definition

Quite arbitrarily, juvenile delinquency is defined for the purposes of this book as illegal behavior by youths. This definition is adopted in the face of recognition that the formal rules that are reflected in the operation of the legal system of the society are not reflected necessarily in the informal moral codes of all segments of the society. The use of forbidden substances (alcohol, marijuana, or other nonprescription drugs,) vandalism, thievery, interpersonal assault, and other activities legally defined as delinquent may be regarded as quite acceptable or consistent with the values of certain youth groups the members of which are of one or the other gender or reside in particular localities. Nevertheless, since the activities are contrary to the legal norms, these behaviors are appropriate objects of consideration in this book.

It is also recognized that, by this definition, the kinds of activities that illustrate juvenile delinquency in a particular society would change over time as the laws governing the behaviors of youths change. If this book on juvenile delinquency were written prior to 1914, it would have no intrinsic interest in the question of why youths in the United States use opiates since use of opiates became illegal in this country only with the passage of the Harrison Stamp Tax Act in 1914. At that time, the behavior became illegal, and people who performed the behavior became criminal. At that point in time, also, it became reasonable to ask why people performed this act that was defined as criminal. Part of the answer may have been that they did not think it was wrong whatever the law said. Part of the answer may have been that they did not think the law could be enforced. Part of the answer could be that they did not respect the law in general and, indeed, they wished to show contempt for the law. In any case, the definition of the act as illegal (for youths as well as adults) justified it being an object of inquiry within the frame of reference of this book.

The purpose of this book is not to consider the social antecedents and consequences of all behavior but only of behavior that is illegal particularly when performed by youths. In defining this as the proper area of inquiry for this volume, no moral judgments are made about the behavior. I simply carve out a set of phenomena for study from the sociological perspective—namely, behaviors that are in violation of legal norms applicable to youths.

SOURCES OF DATA

The study of juvenile delinquency from the sociological point of view requires information regarding the social behaviors, experiences (including the responses of other people), and characteristics (including social identities) of the people who commit delinquent acts. It also requires similar information about the people who do not commit delinquent acts with whom the delinquents are compared. These data are used as indicators of sociological concepts that are interpreted as influences upon and consequences of delinquent behavior. In order to make valid generalizations about the antecedents and consequences of delinquent behavior, such data must be available and must reflect truly the sociological concepts. Such data as they pertain to those who commit juvenile delinquency and to comparison groups can be derived from at least three sources.

Official Records

First, official reports of the criminal incident and of any subsequent arrest and adjudication proceedings can be examined. Such information as is available from these records can be used to describe the individual. Such data might include the sex, race, and previous offenses of the youth. From the point of view of knowing about the person, this is highly unsatisfactory. The official records are not likely to contain information on the person's motives, perceptions of the chances of being caught, attitudes towards society, or any of a number of other things that might help to explain why a youth committed a delinquent act.

In addition, there are a number of other reasons for dissatisfaction with the use of official statistics to learn about those who commit crime. Not all crimes that are committed are discovered and reported to official agencies. Of those that are reported, not all of the ensuing investigations result in arrests. These circumstances would in themselves pose no problem for the purpose of understanding the characteristics of people who are presumed to have committed offenses if the people who are arrested were a representative sample of those who actually committed the crimes. It is quite possible, however, that those who are arrested are not a representative sample of those who committed crimes but rather represent those who are most likely to be caught or (perhaps unjustly) accused of committing crimes. It is possible that the characteristics of individuals arrested for crimes which would be statistically associated with the performance of criminal acts reflect more the chances of getting caught rather than circumstances leading to the commission of deviant acts. It is possible, for example, that blacks and whites may be equally likely to commit delinquent acts but that blacks are more likely to be arrested for committing the acts. Hence, official statistics showing a preponderance of blacks relative to their numbers in the population committing delinquent acts would be interpreted as suggesting that blacks are more likely to commit delinquent acts rather than to be arrested for committing delinquent act. While this might in fact be the case (Hindelang et al., 1981), the source of the data might also mask the degree of racial discrimination in criminal justice processing that contributes to the observed differences in rates of delinquency.

Surveys of Victims

A second source of information that might explain why youths commit delinquent acts is surveys of the population to determine who were victims of delinquent acts. In such surveys the victims could be asked questions regarding the circumstances of the delinquent act and the apparent characteristics of the perpetrators of the act. However, quite apart from other issues such as delinquent acts that have no personal victim (vandalism of public buildings, for example), this source of data provides minimal information regarding possible explanatory factors such as motivation and perceptions of the delinquent youth. Although surveys of victims might provide information regarding opportunity, other important explanatory factors would not be able to be considered.

Self-Reports of Delinquency

Third, an important source of information that might be of explanatory value in accounting for delinquent behavior is self-report studies. That is, individuals are questioned whether or not they performed varieties of delinquent acts and about circumstances that are thought to be relevant to the explanation of the act or of its consequences. For the purpose of explaining delinquent behavior, this technique appears potentially most valuable for providing the kinds of data that are thought to be relevant to accounting for delinquency and its consequences. Nevertheless, self-report studies have been objected to on a number of grounds. Perhaps the most important of these was that the data supplied by youths regarding such sensitive matters as violations of the law could not be trusted to be factual. Further, among those who trusted the relationships derived from official statistics, it was pointed out that results derived from self-report studies did not support the relationships derived from studies of official records. Careful studies of self-report data, however, have come to the conclusion that

with some apparently minor exceptions, the results of self-report research did not behave as though there was something basically wrong. For one thing, the substantive findings of self-report studies were remarkably consistent over time, place, and procedure. For another, the reliability and even validity estimates for self-report instruments were often well within the range of acceptability for social science management. Finally, and perhaps most important, the major problem of self-report measures of crime and delinquency, that they produced findings descrepant from those produced by independent procedures (both official and victimization data), seemed to us to be amenable to a simple solution: If the content of self-report instruments, the delinquent and criminal offenses measured by such instruments, were taken into account, there need be and indeed would be no discrepancy between self-report results, on the one hand, and official data and victimization survey results, on the other [Hindelang et al., 1981: 10].

Since the purpose of this volume is in large part to explain the antecedents and consequences of deviant behavior, the data that are used to provide substantiation for theoretical premises will be derived primarily from self-report research although, on occasion, results of analyses of official data and surveys of victims will also be relevant as will data gained from other sources (such as direct observation) that are not as common in contemporary research on juvenile delinquency.

It is emphasized, however, that the purpose of this volume is to explain the onset, continuity, and consequences of delinquent behavior rather than to estimate the amounts and distribution of the behavior. The acceptance of data based upon one or another research procedure may well provide (as I believe it does) a valid basis for conclusions regarding antecedents and consequences of delinquency without accepting the validity of these techniques for producing veridical findings regarding the levels of various kinds of delinquent behavior among the population at large or among segments of the population.

THEORY AND RESEARCH

In order to develop a continually more effective understanding of the social antecedents and consequences of juvenile delinquency, it is necessary to move back and forth between the processes of constructing theories that guide and are revised in accordance with research findings and the research enterprise that estimates the extent to which theoretical statements reflect reality.

Theory Construction

By the end of this volume, it will be clear that the general processes that lead to and are consequences of delinquent behavior are complex ones and are still only incompletely understood. It is only in relatively recent times that the true complexity of the explanation of delinquency and its consequences has been recognized. Only in the past few years has widespread understanding existed of (1) the large number of variables that play a part in explaining juvenile delinquency and its consequences; (2) the more or less indirect influence of these variables; (3) the possible counteracting influences of a variable whereby the same factor might have some consequences that in turn increase the likelihood of delinquency, and have other consequences that influence the inhibition of delinquency; and (4) the modifier effects of certain variables whereby the effects of another variable upon delinquency are only observed when the modifier variable is present (or absent) or at a particular level.

Contemporary with the recognition of the complexity of these processes, students of delinquency (and, more generally, of deviant behaviors) have constructed complex systems of interrelated propositions (theories) that purport to reflect the reality of the social processes that influence the onset and continuity of delinquency and that are the consequences of delinquency. Toward the goal of understanding delinquency, the building of such theories serves two purposes.

Interpretation of Data

Prior to the development of complex theories of delinquency, a good deal of empirical research was carried out that was either not guided by theory at all or was guided by theories that did not recognize the complexity of reality. As a result, a large sociological literature exists that relates sociocultural variables to deviant behavior in general and to delinquent behavior in particular. Among the more prominent sociocultural variables that have been studied in relationship to delinquent behavior are race, ethnicity, social class, gender, and age.

Such variables are organizing characteristics of the social system. They relate to the structure of the system. Other variables that have been studied relate more to processes by which the system either functions while retaining its present form or changes its structure. Such variables as socialization processes and rates of social change have also been related to delinquency.

However, in the absence of theoretical guidelines, where a relationship was observed between a social variable and delinquency, it could not be determined whether the relationship was a direct or indirect one, under what conditions the relationship held, and the meaning of the relationship. If gender, for example, was observed to be related to juvenile delinquency, was that because males were more likely to fail to reach their expectations, because delinquent patterns were more congruent with masculine roles, because males were more likely to be members of peer subcultures that endorsed delinquent patterns, or because females were more likely to be emotionally attached to representatives of the conventional order and were more likely to be sensitive to interpersonal sanctions, or because of all of these reasons and many others besides? A theoretical framework provides a structure for offering tentative interpretations of the data that then may be subjected to empirical testing.

Identifying Gaps in Understanding

Since theoretical statements represent provisional models of reality, the examination of the degree to which the theory corresponds to empirical observation serves to indicate the adequacy or inadequacy of the theory. The investigator is made sensitive to the need for revision of the theory. As Tittle (1980: 193) noted in connection with a study considering the deterrent effects of fear of sanction upon social deviance:

> The results point clearly to the need for better theory. Perhaps there are other variables that might be identified or perhaps some of the psychological variables that sociologists discount are necessary to achieve effective explanation . . . , but it may also be that we simply need to fit together in a more meaningful way the theory fragments . . . . Despite the penchant of social scientists for one-variable theories we simply must be more eclectic and produce an integrated theory that accommodates a range of variables and specifies the contingencies under which various behavior outcomes are to be expected.

Empirical Testing

Since theoretical models of juvenile delinquency are becoming complex by (1) incorporating a large number of variables, (2) specifying more or less direct and conditional relationships, and (3) indicating the existence of counteracting effects, empirical tests of these theoretical statements should be equal to the task of estimating the complex relationships that in fact are to be observed among a large number of variables.

While such studies are not yet common (as formulations of complex theories of delinquency are relatively rare), analyses of more or less direct and conditional relationships among a large number of variables said to be associated with juvenile delinquency do exist. For example, Richard Johnson (1979) tested a complex model of juvenile delinquency using data collected in 1975 from 734 sophomores in three high schools located in relatively poor areas of Seattle. The analysis was a relatively sophisticated one as measured against existing studies of juvenile delinquency. The study was theoretically based and included a broad range of mutually influential factors that are suspected to play a role in the development of juvenile delinquency.

A limitation of the study and of other similar studies, however, is the inability to establish the sequences in time of the factors that are thought to cause and to be consequences of juvenile delinquency. Since the data were collected at the same point in time, it could only be assumed that, for example, having delinquent associates preceded delinquent behavior in time (rather than that delinquent behaviors led the youth subsequently to seek out associates who also performed delinquent acts) or that having failing grades caused a later decreased attachment to school (rather than that the decreased attachment to school caused the person to try less hard and, consequently, to fail in school). Johnson was only able to assume certain sequences of events and to examine whether the observations fit the assumptions that he made.

More recent studies have used longitudinal data (Kaplan et al., 1982, 1984). Since the data were collected at different points in time, the sequences of events could be established with greater credibility. Like the Johnson (1979) study, the more recent investigations try to test complex theories that incorporate the presumed effects of a large number of variables on each other and on juvenile delinquency. A further advantage in these studies, however, is the ability to establish with more credibility that certain variables precede or follow other variables that more or less directly (and conditionally) influence the onset of juvenile delinquency. Such theoretically based, multivariate, longitudinal studies show promise of greatly increasing our understanding of the onset, continuity, and consequences of juvenile delinquency in the near future.

In the following chapters, I will cite findings from these relatively rare studies where it seems appropriate to do so. However, I will also make good use of studies that are more limited in scope and that employ cross-sectional rather than longitudinal research designs. The results of these studies also will contribute to the tentative formulation of a theoretical model that appears to reflect the complexity of the social processes that stimulate and issue from patterns of juvenile delinquency.

SUMMARY

Juvenile delinquency is defined as behaviors by youths that violate laws that are applicable to that age group. Because delinquency reflects behaviors, they should be studied with reference to the same general principles that are used to study more inclusive categories of behavior. Delinquency as behavior is distinguished from the social attitudes toward the behavior that are often confused with it. Delinquency refers specifically to age-related violations of law. Although some behaviors are illegal for all age-groups, other behaviors as well may be illegal only for youths. Juvenile delinquency is defined in terms of legal rather than moral definitions. It is possible for certain acts to be illicit from the current perspective of legal institutions and yet be morally acceptable among certain segments of the population. Over time the legal definition of delinquent behavior may change.

The study of juvenile delinquency depends upon data from a variety of sources including official records, surveys of victims, and self-report studies as well as from other less frequently used sources such as direct observation studies. These data are used to formulate generalizations about the antecedents and consequences of delinquent behavior.

Research on delinquent behavior increasingly is guided by theoretical statements that, in turn, are revised in the face of research findings. Theoretical statements are coming to recognize the complexity of explanations of the antecedents and consequences of deviant behaviors. The complexity is reflected in the number of variables that are involved, the indirect as well as direct influences of one variable upon another, the counteracting influences of one variable upon another, and the conditional nature of relationships between variables. The theoretical structure provides tentative interpretations of research findings and permits identification of areas where further research is needed.

As theoretical statements become more complex, so do research activities become more suitable to the task of testing the theories. Increasingly, research on juvenile delinquency permits analysis of the complex relationships among an appropriately large number of variables using research designs that permit the determination of the temporal sequences of the variables.

DISCUSSION QUESTIONS

1. What general principles that are used to explain behavior in general would be useful in explaining delinquent behavior in particular?

2. What purposes (if any) does it serve for some behaviors to be illegal for youths but to be legal for adults?

3. How might scientific beliefs about delinquency be affected by the sources of the data?

4. Why might a particular variable such as the gender of the youth affect delinquent behavior? Consider how gender might have indirect effects upon delinquency, how it might have some effects that increase and other effects that decrease delinquent behavior, and how gender might have certain effects upon delinquency when certain conditions are present but not under other conditions.

2

SOCIAL DEFINITION OF JUVENILE DELINQUENCY

Social groups make the rules (including laws that define specific acts performed by youths as juvenile delinquency) the violation of which constitutes deviant behavior. It is important to understand the process by which specific behaviors when performed by specified categories of people in specified situations come to be defined as juvenile delinquency because this process is part of the explanation of the onset, continuity and consequences of delinquency.

SOCIAL DEFINITION AS EXPLANATION

Social definition of behavior is part of the explanation of delinquency in the trivial sense that changes in the law would change rates of crime because the behaviors (although they might persist) are no longer labeled (or are now labeled) criminal. However, I ignore this understanding of the effect of social definition because it does not address the questions that are the concern of this book—those relating to the causes and effects of the behavior that is defined as delinquent. The preceding observation merely states that if you change the law, you change the labeling of a behavior as criminal.

In a more profound sense, however, the process of defining specified behaviors as delinquent is part of the explanation of delinquent behavior. At various points in the following chapters, we will observe that the fact that certain behaviors are defined as delinquent (1) will serve (under different conditions) to stimulate or inhibit motivation to perform delinquent acts; and (2) will evoke social responses that (depending upon other moderating conditions) influence the continuity, change in level of involvement, or discontinuity of delinquent behavior. Since the social definition of behaviors as delinquency has these effects, it follows that any variables that influence the social definition of behavior as delinquent will have indirect effects upon the onset and continuity of the delinquent behavior. It will be observed also that patterns of delinquent behavior (and, less directly, the causes of delinquent behavior) influence the social definition of the behavior as delinquent. For example, the more prevalent certain patterns of delinquent behavior become, the greater is the pressure to redefine the behavior as within the realm of acceptable responses.

Because the social definition of delinquent behavior is significant in the explanation of the onset, continuity, and consequences of delinquent behavior, I consider briefly the processes that influence the definitional process.

DEFINING DELINQUENCY

The process by which particular behaviors come to be defined as juvenile delinquency cannot be understood apart from a consideration of such major influences as subcultural diversity and political influence.

Subcultural Diversity

In modern society it is not difficult to observe the presence of different, frequently conflicting value systems shared by more or less inclusive segments of the population that have in common regional, racial, ethnic, social class, and perhaps maturational (age or stage of social development) characteristics. In part, the subcultural diversity is the result of the convergence of representatives of foreign culture within common geographic limits. In part, the absence of cultural consensus is the result of rapid and uneven rates of cultural change among different segments of the population thus ensuring that, over time, even among a group that initially shared a value system, diversity of value judgments would emerge.

Political Influence

Surveys of the population suggest that at least occasionally, laws are passed that do not reflect the sentiments of the great majority of the population. In a survey of a sample of subjects in three states, Tittle (1980) found that at least two legally prohibited offenses by implication did not receive overwhelming support. Only 30 percent of the subjects thought gambling was both serious and should be prohibited by law, and only 59 percent of the population saw marijuana smoking as both serious and worthy of legal prohibition. In contrast to these acts, 91 percent of the subjects, 88 percent of the subjects, and 72 percent of the subjects, respectively, judged assault, $50 theft, and $5 theft to be serious and worthy of prohibition by law.

If laws that are contrary to the beliefs of the general population exist, then either such laws are on the verge of change (Tittle, 1980) or groups have wielded political influence out of proportion to their numbers in order to effect the legislation.

According to the second possibility, those segments of the population that differ in the system of values to which each segment subscribes do not exercise equal influence in the formal institutions whereby laws are enacted or enforced. The segments of the population that are more influential are more likely to enact and enforce laws that reflect their concepts of high priority values. Any behaviors that threaten these values, although they may be congruent with the values shared by other less powerful segments of the population, will be defined as delinquent.

The exercise of undue political influence in the passage of legislation that reflects primarily the values of powerful minorities is apparent in the behavioral science literature over the last several decades. This process is nicely illustrated by the report of Lind (1938) on deviant behavior in Hawaii. This report suggests that the westerners in Honolulu represented a politically powerful minority group that was able to legislate patterns that were contrary to the values of other groups. In particular, the high illegitimacy rate among the Polynesians was consistent with the acceptability of premarital sexual activity but was contrary to the values of the politically influential westerners.

Other examples are provided by Thorsten Sellin's (1938) seminal discussion of the relationship between crime and culture conflict. Rich illustrations are provided of processes whereby the legal definition of a crime was initiated and enforced although the definition was compatible with the values of only the influential minority and was incompatible with norms of acceptable behavior shared by other (frequently more numerous, but less powerful) segments of the population.

While the legal structure of society reflects the values of influential segments of the population, the political structure itself develops its own needs and may be prompted to initiate legislation that will serve these needs. Such observations have been made by a large number of sociologists, particularly those who have come to be associated with "labeling theory." Among the more prominent of these was Howard S. Becker (1963) who considered the process by which marijuana use came to be defined as illegal with the passage of the Marijuana Stamp Tax Act of 1937. Becker argued that the "moral entrepreneurs" who succeeded in creating and enforcing new rules defining marijuana use as criminal were the functionaries of the Federal Bureau of Narcotics. The passage of the law was said to be motivated by the felt need of the functionaries to increase their sphere of influence. Passage of the federal felony law was facilitated by a mass media campaign to which the Bureau of Narcotics apparently contributed stories that associated marijuana use with violent behavior.

The recognition of the roles of cultural diversity and political influence in the deviance-defining process is most apparent in the theoretical perspectives known as conflict theory. As Farrell and Swigert (1982: 226-227) summarize this perspective:

> Deviance is the result of social and cultural diversity. Modern society is made up of a proliferation of collectivities, each attempting to satisfy its own needs and promote its standards of value. By gaining access to the institutions of social control, successful competitiors are able to establish their norms and interests as the dominant ones and derogate groups that would challenge their position of superiority. Nonconformity, therefore, is intimately related to the socio-political organization of society. Whether because of the cultural differences found among groups or because of the privileges and obligations that accompany the various levels of class, status, and power, minority populations are subject to deviance-defining processes that render their situation and behavior condemnable.

Although I do not develop this idea here, as the influence of the social definition of delinquency upon the onset and continuity of delinquent behavior becomes apparent in later chapters, the sociocultural diversity and processes of political influence that affect the social definition of juvenile delinquency should be regarded as indirectly influencing the onset and continuity of delinquent behavior. In like manner, as the influence of delinquent behavior upon the social definition of delinquent behavior becomes apparent, cultural diversity and political influence should be viewed as intervening between these two variables.

SUMMARY

The fact that certain behaviors are defined as juvenile delinquency is part of the explanation of whether or not people adopt and continue delinquent patterns, and social definitions of behavior as juvenile delinquency are among the consequences of delinquent behavior.

The social definition of behavior as delinquent stems from the differential ability of socioculturally diverse segments of the population to influence the political process. The definition of particular behaviors as delinquent will be influenced disproportionately by those segments of the population whose values are reflected in and control the offices of the political process.

DISCUSSION QUESTIONS

1. When might the definition of a particular behavior as delinquent increase and when might it decrease the likelihood of future performance of the behavior?

2. What segments of the population are most influential in the definition of behavior as delinquent? In particular, how much influence do youths exercise in the social definition of delinquent behavior?

3. What effects do the mass media exercise on social and cultural diversity? How will these effects influence the extent to which laws influence societywide feelings about which behaviors should be defined as delinquent?

3

MOTIVATION TO COMMIT DELINQUENT ACTS VIOLATING MEMBERSHIP GROUP NORMS

In this chapter I begin to address the question of why young people behave in ways that are proscribed or fail to behave in ways that are prescribed for them by the formal legal system of the society. That is, why do juveniles behave in ways that are judged to be delinquent by the legal system of the more inclusive society? The first set of factors to be considered concerns the person's motivation to perform a delinquent act.

DELINQUENT DISPOSITIONS

A youth is more likely to perform an act that the society (through the operation of the legal system) judges to be delinquent if he anticipates, whether consciously or unconsciously, that some satisfaction of his or her needs will be gained. To say that an individual is disposed or motivated to commit a delinquent act is to say that the act symbolizes for the youth the achievement of a goal and, therefore, the satisfaction of a need to reach the goal.

In this chapter and Chapter 4, I will consider two sets of circumstances that give rise to the motivation to commit delinquent acts and two corresponding sets of satisfactions that are expected to be gained from delinquent acts. In the present chapter I consider the circumstances surrounding the development of dispositions to perform delinquent acts that involve (1) the youth's earlier commitment to the normative system that judged such acts to be wrong and (2) the failure to achieve what was expected of the youth according to the conventional standards. The youth comes to see delinquent patterns in general, or particular delinquent patterns as the only or most promising ways of satisfying his or her unresolved needs that up to now the youth tried to satisfy using more conventional response patterns.

In Chapter 4 I consider the circumstances surrounding the development of dispositions to perform acts that are legally defined as delinquent but nevertheless conform to the expectations of groups to which the youth belongs or wishes to belong. The delinquent behaviors reflect the values of these groups. The youth is motivated to perform these delinquent behaviors that reflect group norms in order to gain the satisfactions associated with the behaviors themselves, the approval of other group members for performing the behaviors, and the youth's identification with a positive reference group. Before considering these circumstances in greater detail, however, I return to a more detailed consideration of the circumstances leading to the failure to achieve conventional values and the associated development of dispositions toward delinquent responses.

CONVENTIONAL FAILURE AND DEVIANT DISPOSITIONS

In the course of the normal socialization process experienced by the individual, the youth learns to value the possession of particular attributes, the performance of certain behaviors, and particular experiences that are the outcome of the purposive or accidential responses of others toward the youth. These attributes, behaviors, and experiences, are the basis for the youth's feelings of self-worth. If the person is unable to evaluate himself or herself positively, then the youth will be motivated to behave in ways that will gain the attributes, enable the performance of the behaviors, and increase the likelihood of the experiences that will increase feelings of self-worth and decrease the feelings of psychological distress that are associated with self-rejecting attitudes. If the youth perceives an inability to achieve the attributes, perform the behaviors, and enjoy the experiences he or she has been taught to value as the basis for overall positive self-evaluation through conventional behavior, then the youth will be motivated to behave in deviant ways that offer promise of gaining attributes, facilitating behaviors, and enjoying experiences that will permit the youth to gain a feeling of self-worth. The deviant behavior may involve using illegal means to achieve what the youth has learned to value or engaging in illegal activities as a way of rejecting the conventional standards by which one failed and substituting illegitimate standards by which the youth could more easily succeed and earn feelings of self-worth.

This brief formulation of the process by which individuals become disposed to perform delinquent acts that violate the moral codes of the groups in which they were raised is a reflection of a theoretical and research tradition in which motives to perform delinquent acts are viewed as attempts to adjust to the psychological distress associated with failures to achieve specific values such as parental acceptance or occupational success. In the preceding synopsis and synthesis of this tradition, I merely subsumed the various specific motives that are attributed to youths (individually or collectively) as presumed antecedents of deviant response under a more general motive— the need to avoid self-rejecting attitudes and to maintain or promote positive self-attitudes. Specific motives to attain by illegitimate means consensually valued goals are accounted for by the need to feel positively toward oneself, a prerequisite for which is the achievement of the consensually valued goals. Motivated acts that reflect contempt for the conventional value system and endorsement of values that contradict conventional value systems are intended to function in the service of the self-esteem motive by destroying the validity of the standards by which the person failed and, therefore, which required self-devaluing responses. Delinquent patterns that appear to be motivated by, the need to retreat (whether by decreasing contact with others or changing one's psychological state) from contact with the conventional value structure function to enhance self-attitudes by (1) avoiding continuing experiences of failure and rejection when measured against conventional standards, or (2) avoiding recognition of such failure and rejection. The attraction of individuals who were socialized according to conventional values to groups that endorse delinquent values in addition to serving any of the foregoing self-enhancing functions, provides a new set of (delinquent) standards that the person can adopt, achieve, and, therefore, use as a basis for positive self-evaluation (Kaplan, 1972, 1975, 1980, 1982).

I now turn to a consideration of the theoretical and empirical literature that in greater detail considers the nature of the conventional failures experienced by youths, aspects of social structure and process that increase the likelihood of conventional failure, and the association between these variables and delinquent behavior.

Earlier Theoretical Formulations

A number of theories and the empirical studies based on these explain deviant behavior (including juvenile delinquency) in terms of motivation to achieve certain goals or to meet certain needs that can only or best be met through deviant response patterns. The delinquent patterns may be intrinsically valued (the satisfaction to be gained from the behavior is in the behavior itself) or may be instrumentally valued (the delinquent behavior is a way of getting something else that the person values). Various social conditions are said to account for the failure of individuals to reach their goals except through the use of delinquent patterns. Such theories are best illustrated by strain and subculture theories.

Anomic Strain

Among the more prominent of the theories of this type is that presented by Merton (1957) as an extension of some of Durkheim's earlier writings. From this perspective, deviant behavior is a response to *anomie*. Anomie is "a breakdown in the social structure, occurring particularly when there is an acute disjunction between the cultural norms and goals and the socially structured capacities of members of the group to act in accord with them" (Merton, 1957: 162). The individual experiences the breakdown in the cultural structure as anomic strain, which is adapted to in any of a number of deviant ways. From the point of view of explaining juvenile delinquency, the most significant of these modes of adaptations is *innovation,* where the person continues to value highly the goals of society but rejects the conventional means for reaching these goals that he does not have access to. In order to reach desirable goals, he reaches out and uses illegitimate means. Juvenile delinquency among the poor reflects an attempt to reach socially valued economic affluence or other culturally defined goals through illegitimate means. The poor have been taught to want the same things as other strata but do not have the same degree of access to the resources that are required for success in reaching those goals. Hence, the poor are more likely to seek and adopt illicit alternative means to the achievement of the goals.

Critics of this position, often known as "structured strain" or simply "strain" theory, have pointed out that social class position has not been consistently observed to vary with delinquent acts (Johnson, 1979). If this is the case, then the disjunction between conventional goals and available conventional means that supposedly characterizes the lower class cannot be taken as an explanation of delinquency. However, the absence of an empirical association between lower social class position and delinquent behavior by itself cannot be taken as a refutation of this theory. First, it might be argued that the inability to achieve particular conventional goals through conventional means is observed disproportionately in the lower class. Second, it might also be argued plausibly that the lower class who experience the failure to achieve the conventional goals because of the absence of conventional resources are indeed motivated to engage in illicit activities. However, this is not to say necessarily that other social classes are not equally vulnerable to circumstances that prevent them from achieving personally valued goals and that, therefore, dispose them to engage in delinquent acitivites. The frustration of not achieving their valued goals (although different from those that the lower class youths fail to achieve) are as meaningful as stimuli to illicit activities to the members of higher social classes as is the frustration of not achieving the values experienced by members of the lower class. Thus, all classes may experience equivalent frustration (and, therefore, equivalent dispositions to engage in delinquent behavior) because of the failure to achieve different socially valued goals. In this connection it should also be pointed out that the goals may be the same, but the ways in which the achievement of the goals is evaluated may vary according to social class and so result in equivalent levels of frustration, although by absolute standards the higher classes have less reason to be frustrated. Thus, the lower class may measure their own success against the achievement of the other classes and so feel frustrated, while the middle classes judge themselves against the standards of achievement of the privileged few and feel similarly frustrated.

In any case, whenever the frustration is apparent (perhaps reflected in low expectation of future success), regardless of social class, that frustration tends to be associated with delinquent dispositions. Consistent with this position, Elliott (1961) found that in both the middle and lower classes, low expectations of future success are associated with delinquency.

An alternative explanation for the failure to observe social class-related differences in delinquent behavior that would still permit acceptance of the basic tenets of the anomic strain perspective is based on the distinction between the motivation to engage in delinquent behavior and the acting-out of the motives. It is possible that members of the lower social class, for the reasons specified in strain theory, do become more disposed than other members of society to engage in delinquent acts but are more likely (for reasons not yet understood) to forego acting out deviant impulses.

Subculture Theory

The idea that delinquent behaviors reflect responses to the failure to achieve conventional goals through conventional means is apparent in a number of theoretical formulations described as subculture theories. These formulations concern the origin and functioning of subcultures in which delinquent acitivites are endorsed. The forms of adaptive response might take any of a number of forms. Various students of gang delinquency have suggested different adaptive processes. Implicit in Sutherland's (1937) descriptions of behavior systems of crime, Shaw and McKay's (1942) discussion of criminal traditions in high delinquency areas, and Cloward and Ohlin's (1960) identification of criminal subcultures is the notion that the subcultures arose in response to the need to achieve the success goals endorsed by the conventional society but through the use of illegitimate means that were the only effective means available to those who formed or joined criminal subcultures. The goals were conventional ones, but the patterns used to achieve the goals (becoming professional criminals) were illegitimate.

Albert K. Cohen (1955) suggested that the inability of youths to achieve the middle-class values that they had learned in the course of the socialization process resulted in a different form of adaptation. Rather than accept the worth of the conventional values and adopt illegitimate means to the achievement of these values, youths collectively *reject* the worth of the values by their endorsement of values that are the exact opposite of those endorsed by conventional society. If they cannot succeed in achieving one set of values, they will judge the values to be not worth achieving and will act accordingly. As Kobrin describes this process, as a result of the failure to achieve the symbols of success in the dominant middle class culture, youths are exposed to negative evaluative judgments by the representatives of that middle-class culture with whom the youths come into contact.

> One of several adaptive responses available to young males in this situation is to reject the imputation of inferiority and degradation by emphasizing those activities and personal traits which distinguish them from striving, upward mobile persons. The common response inaugurates new norms of conduct out of which develop the distinctive criteria of status in the delinquent group. Thus a coherent social milieu is created in which status is distributed according to success in attacking the symbol of middle-class respectability. Since property represents a central symbol of merit and virtue in the culture of this class, stealing and destructiveness become a principal though not the only form taken by the attack [1951: 659].

The subcultural adoption described by Cohen (1955) and Kobrin (1951) appears similar to the conflict subculture identified later by Cloward and Ohlin (1960).

The analysis of data collected by a self-administered anonymous questionnaire from 734 sophomores in three Seattle, Washington, high schools during April 1975 seems to support the conclusion that certain types of delinquency reflect such a total rejection of the evaluative standards according to which the youths would have to describe themselves as failures (Johnson, 1979). Vandalism rather than theft and assault most clearly reflect symbolic contempt for conventional social institutions. Lower social class position and/or low expectations of future occupational success reflects inability to judge oneself positively according to conventional standards of success. Thus, consistent with the hypothesis that failure according to conventional standards leads to a rejection of the validity of these standards, for both white males and white females, being a member of the underclass tended to be associated with acts of vandalism but not with acts of theft or assault. Further, for white females low occupational expectations tended to be associated with acts of vandalism but not with acts of theft or assault.

Another collective adaptation to the failure to successfully achieve conventional values described by Cloward and Ohlin (1960) is the formation of drug subcultures that permit youths in urban slum areas to withdraw from the conventional value system in response to the absence of opportunities (whether legitimate or illegitimate) to achieve these values.

Once the subcultures have been established, they represent opportunities for the individual who is disposed to delinquent activities to achieve conventional satisfactions through illicit means or to achieve alternative nonconventional satisfactions. The potential satisfactions to be derived from participating in a street-addict subculture have been described by a social-psychologist as follows:

> Specifically, the addict gets three things out of his involvement with narcotics. First, he gains an identify, posing little to live up to. Second, he gains a place in a subsociety where he is unequivocally accepted as a peer, a not too demanding place among his fellow men, a segment of society where he fits and belongs. Third, he acquires a career at which he is reasonably competent. [Chein, 1966: 65].

Empirical Findings

Findings from multivariate cross-sectional and longitudinal studies support the theoretical positions that failure to achieve such conventional goals as success in school, loving responses from parents, and the self-respect to which these achievements contribute, leads to deviant dispositions. The deviant dispositions are variously reflected in negative attitudes toward conventional patterns (alienation), the attraction to deviant standards, and the actual performance of delinquent acts.

Alienation from the Conventional Environment

Findings reported by Kaplan and his associates (1984) are consistent with the idea that the loss of motivation to conform to normative standards and the development of motivation to deviate from normative standards is a consequence of earlier feelings of being rejected by conventional groups and of feelings of self-rejection developed in the course of membership group experiences. These findings are particularly interesting since the measures of alienation from the conventional environment were taken at a later point in time than the measures of self-rejecting feelings and feelings of being rejected according to family and school standards. Measures of self-rejecting feelings, in turn, were predicted by feelings of alienation from the conventional environment (partly reflected in the expectations of not being able to achieve according to conventional standards in the future) and past feelings of being rejected according to family and school standards.

Delinquent Associates

The failure of an individual to achieve self-esteem through success according to conventional adult standards may lead him to search for such esteem through alternative deviant standards. The attraction to such standards is reflected in increased association with those who conform to them.

Numerous studies point to having delinquent friends as one of the major factors in delinquent behavior. Whether or not the youth has friends who are delinquent, however, appears to depend upon how closely they are tied to the conventional social institutions, particularly the school. Youths who think grades, what their teachers think of them, education, and homework are important, who like and try hard in school, are less likely to have delinquent associates (Johnson, 1979). Those people who are attached to school are youths who have succeeded according to conventional values. They have been successful in school and have evoked loving and converned responses from their parents.

Kaplan and his associates (1984) reported that the perception of deviant opportunities (the awarness that many of the kids at school perform delinquent acts) is preceded by feelings of being rejected according to the standards of the family and the school. However, the relationships are significant only for youths whose parents had moderate or high levels of education. These findings are consistent with the notion that individuals who fail by conventional standards will be more likely to become aware of deviant standards.

Delinquent Behavior

Longitudinal data collected from several thousand junior high school students in Houston supported the hypothesis that past inability to achieve and expectations of future inability to achieve socially valued goals lead to the performance of deviant acts. A measure of alienation taken in the seventh grade was associated with reports of deviant behavior in the eighth grade after controlling for reports of deviant behavior in the seventh grade as well as other variables (Kaplan et al., 1984).

Other data from the same study (Kaplan and Robbins, 1983) found that a measure of the youth's perceived failure according to school standards (by my teachers' standards I am a failure; my teachers do not like me very much; I probably will not go to school and graduate; and so on) was a consistent indicator of subsequent adoption of delinquent behaviors. Felt rejection in the school setting predicted theft, coming into contact with police, carrying weapons, engaging in illegal drug traffic, using illicit drugs, and other delinquent acts. Only those youths who denied performance of these acts during the preceding year were included in the analysis. The relationship between felt rejection in the school environment and delinquent behaviors was observed after controlling for a number of other theoretically indicated antecedents of delinquent behavior. Further, not only did *level* of experiences of rejection in the school environment predict subsequent adoption of delinquent behavior patterns, but *increases* in feelings of being rejected according to school standards predicted later performance of deviant behavior as well.

Social Determinants of Conventional Failure

A good deal of literature is consistent with the view that motivation to perform deviant acts among youths who were raised to accept conventional values and rules can be traced to the failure of the youths to achieve conventional goals through the use of conventional resources. The inability to achieve what the youth is expected to achieve may be thought of in terms of the expectations being too great for the resources that the person has, or in terms of the resources being too few to achieve what is expected. It does not matter if the youth has great expectations if the person has resources that are adequate to reach the expectations. It is only when the resources are too few that the expectations are too high; and it is when the expectations are too high that, in effect, the resources are too low.

How then does it happen that aspirations are too high for available resources? The answer to this question concerns (among other factors) roles associated with particular social indentities that define the demands made upon the youth and the resources that are available to the youth, normative life events involving changes in social positions and the relative increase in demands upon the youth or decreases in resources with which to meet the demands, and social change in the role definitions associated with particular identities that may have similar effects.

Social Positions

Sociologists have speculated about a large number of social positions both with regard to the differences in the obligations imposed upon people who occupy those positions and the resources available to them with which they can meet the demands.

The differences in demands made upon those with different social identities may be illustrated by positions differentiated according to gender. For example, it has been argued in the past (Hewitt, 1970) that for working-class boys, occupational values are more important than for working-class girls. Since school success is frequently required for success in occupational areas, failure in school would be more threatening to boys than to girls for whom occupational aspirations are less important and, therefore, for whom the prospects of failure in school are less threatening. If they do not aspire to occupational success, they they would not be threatened by any prospective school failure that is prerequisite to that success.

If in fact school failure is more significant for boys than for girls, then it is to be expected that delinquent dispositions would be more likely to arise for boys who failed than for girls who failed and, of course, boys would, therefore, be more likely to commit delinquent acts than girls in response to failure. In fact, Johnson did observe that there is a sex difference

in the magnitude of effects of school performance among both whites and Asians. That is, failure in schools has a much greater delinquency-producing effect for boys than for girls. . . . School success is evidently not as large a portion of a girl's stake in conformity and therefore not as relevant to their delinquent involvement [1979: 127-128].

With regard to resources, sociologists have long considered that social class position, for example, will determine whether or not the youth will have such resources as supportive parents, academic values, financial aid, educational background, family influence, and even physical health.

Normative Life Events

Whenever the person's social experiences lead him to the experience of failure or to the belief that he or she will probably fail to achieve what is expected of him, the youth is more likely to adopt delinquent responses in an attempt to prevent or reduce the expeience of failure. Such experiences are increasingly likely when the person experiences certain life events that, although they may be expected, have implications for increasing the demands made upon the youth (without necessarily increasing resources) or for decreasing resources (without necessarily decreasing obligations.) The resulting experience of failure stemming from inability to meet role obligations increases the probability of developing motivations to perform delinquent acts. Winick, for example, argues that

> all points of taking on new roles or all points of being tested for adequacy in a role are likely to be related to role strain and thus to a greater incidence of drug dependence in a group. We also hypothesize that incompatible demands within one role, such as between two roles in the same role set, are likely to lead to a greater incidence of drug dependence [1980: 226].

Consistent with this reasoning, he notes the conclusion of a large scale study (Winick, 1964) to the effect that the onset of addiction

> was concentrated during the years of late adolescence and early adulthood because of the role strain stemming from

decisions about sex, adult responsibility, social relationships, family situations, school, and work, as well as from role deprivation resulting from the loss of familiar patterns of behavior [Winick, 1980: 226].

He found that whatever the age at which youths were allowed to work (and this varies from state to state), that age tended to be the age at which there was a peak of new cases of drug dependence. He also cited a report (Winick and Goldstein, 1964) that indicated glue sniffing to be highest among youths who were entering junior high school. Other twelve-year olds who did not go on to junior high school but rather stayed in an eight-year elementary school showed much less glue sniffing. Again, these findings suggest that the youths who were about to start on a work career or to enter a new environment (junior high school) were fearful of not being able to do what was to be expected of them.

Changing Role Definitions

The influence of social changes in role definitions on the youth's ability to conform to role-related obligations, and the influence of the failure to meet these legitimate expectations on the development of delinquent dispositions may be reflected in social changes that perhaps are occurring in gender-related role definitions.

Social changes over the past few decades, suggest that occupational aspirations (and by implication the need to succeed in school which is necessary to reach occupational goals) may be rising for women. Further, it is not unreasonable to suggest that the expectations have risen more quickly than the ability to fulfill those expectations. Certainly, it is conventional wisdom that more obstacles are placed in the paths of women than in the paths of men on their way to financial and occupational success. The anticipation of such failure might increasingly lead to the disposition to delinquent orientations and ultimately to delinquent behavior on the part of women. The decreasing sex ratio in rates of delinquency that has been observed over the last few decades (Hindelang et al., 1981) is consistent with the interpretations that increased aspirations in the absence of corresponding increases in resources (that is, access to educational experience and occupational advancement) leads women to anticipate that they will fail to achieve what they now believe are appropriate expectations for them. The sense of failure generates deviant dispositions to behave in ways that will achieve conventional goals through illicit means, will question the worth of conventional values, or will substitute different (delinquent) values that are more easily achieved.

SUMMARY

Part of the explanation of why youths perform acts that are delinquent by social standards is that they are motivated to perform these behaviors. They have needs that they feel can best be met by performing the delinquent behaviors. A number of these needs arise because the youth has been unable to meet the expectations that others and the youth himself feel he should meet. He does not possess the valued qualities, perform the appropriate behaviors, or have the desirable experiences that contribute to his feelings of self-worth. The youth becomes motivated to perform delinquent acts because of the need to restore feelings of self-worth. The delinquent behaviors contribute to these feelings of self-worth by attacking the worth of the values according to the standards of which the youth was judged unworthy, by permitting withdrawal from the conventional value system according to the standards of which the youth was a failure, or by permitting the substitution of new (deviant) standards that are more easily achieved than the earlier conventional ones. The specific satisfactions that are expected to derive from delinquent behaviors are specified in theories centering on anomic strain and the development of subcultures as responses to the failure to achieve conventional values.

Research findings support the position that the failure to have valued experiences, achieve valued attributes, and perform conventionally valued behaviors in the social groups in which they were socialized leads to motivation to perform delinquent acts. The deviant motivations in these studies are reflected in feelings of alienation from conventional patterns, attraction to delinquent standards, and the actual performance of delinquent acts.

The failure to achieve according to conventional standards is the result of the levels and kinds of expectations or values being too high for the resources that the youth has at his or her disposal to achieve the values, or of the resources being too few for the achievement of the conventional standards. The levels of expectations or aspirations and the available resources to reach those standards are part of the role definitions and circumstances surrounding the youth's occupying particular social positions. Thus, the demands made upon the youth and the ability to meet those demands will be profoundly influenced by the youth's various social identities, normative life events that mandate changes in social identities and the roles that define them, and social changes in the role definition of particular social identities.

DISCUSSION QUESTIONS

1. What kinds of qualities, behaviors, or experiences do young people value most highly and contribute most to feelings of self-worth?

2. What circumstances are most likely to prevent a person from having these qualities, performing these behaviors, and having these experiences?

3. Has there been any change over the past ten or twenty years in the kinds of things that have been expected of young people? Have there been any changes in the abilities of young people to do what is expected of them over the same period of time?

4. Think of the family as if it were a society, and of the family rules as if they were laws. Does consistent failure of children to do what is expected of them lead them to be motivated to perform acts that violate family rules? What forms might such behavior take? How might these behaviors satisfy the youth's needs?

4

MOTIVATION TO COMMIT DELINQUENT ACTS CONFORMING TO MEMBERSHIP GROUP NORMS

In the preceding chapter I discussed motivation to perform delinquent acts that are not only legally defined as delinquent but also reflect violations of norms that the youth learned in the course of socialization in his groups. The youth developed dispositions to perform delinquent acts because of a need to reduce feelings of self-rejection stemming from being unable to measure up to social and personal values. In this chapter I consider motivation to perform acts that, although they are legally defined as delinquent, nevertheless conform to the standards of groups to which the youth belongs or aspires to belong.

DELINQUENT SUBCULTURES

The systems of standards that are shared by segments of a more inclusive population defined in terms of social characteristics and, frequently, geographic boundaries will be called subcultures. Where the standards include endorsements of behaviors that are legally defined as delinquent, whether or not they also include endorsements of nondelinquent patterns, the system of standards will be labelled a *delinquent* subculture. If the fact that the endorsed patterns of behavior are legally defined as delinquent is recognized at all by those who share the subculture, these people judge the legal norms to be either inapplicable to them or at least less morally binding than the more informal normative expectations that do guide the behavior of those who share the normative expectations comprising the subculture.

In Chapter 3 a number of delinquent subcultures were introduced in connection with a discussion of the range of satisfactions that delinquent ways of life promise to those who developed feelings of failure in the course of life in conventional groups. These delinquent groups vary in the extent to which the delinquent patterns that are endorsed influence the other response patterns. In some delinquent subcultures, the delinquent behavior is the centerpiece of the normative system, influencing virtually every aspect of the subculture. In the subculture of the professional criminal, as an illustration, illicit activities are closely associated with the language, interpersonal associations, and general life style. Sutherland (1937), for example, observed systems of behavior ("behavior systems of crime") among professional thieves. These systems of behavior (what would later be termed "subcultures of deviance" by others) develop out of patterns of differential association whereby the criminals associate with each other more than they do with noncriminals and in the process develop a common argot and other response patterns that are passed on to others as they become associated with the professional thieves. The illicit activity itself is the basis of the differential association and the shared meanings.

In other subcultures, however, the delinquent acts appear to be incidental to everyday life activities. Although the youths may perform a number of illegal activities, the shared norms of the members of the gang pertain to a whole range of activities that in themselves are not illegal whether or not they may deviate from the expectations of the more influental representatives of society. These activities include leisure activities; relationships with the family, school, and other authorities; interaction between the sexes; and economic pursuits. Furthermore, the delinquent activities that reflect sub-cultural values such as risk-taking might easily be substituted for in the minds of the youths that share the culture. While delinquent activities might reflect the shared values of daring or toughness because of their association with risk of apprehension by police, so might other activities that in themselves are not illegal such as boxing, skydiving, or other behaviors that carry with them great risk of physical injury. Feldman's research, for example, illustrates nicely how an illicit activity is not meaningful in itself but only as a reflection of other values. In attempting to account for the movement of the slum youth into a pattern of drug experimentation, Feldman (1968) points to the significance of the social definitions of the slum environment with regard to how prestige may be won or lost. According to the slum neighborhood ideology, high-status reputations are earned by conforming to behavior patterns that are represented in the ideal type of the "stand-up cat." In order to achieve this kind of reputation, situations must arise or be sought out in which the candidate, "can prove his daring, strength, predilection for excitement, and ultimate toughness" (p. 133). The introduction of drug use into the neighborhood is said to offer such an opportunity. Thus, it is asserted that in the slum environment initial experimentation with drugs is a way of achieving prestige:

> The user turns to drugs. . . to capitalize on a new mode of enhancing his status and prestige within a social system where the highest prizes go to persons who demonstrate attributes of toughness, daring, and adventure. Within the life-style of the stand-up-cat, movement into heroin use is one route to becoming a "somebody" in the eyes of the important people who comprise the slum social network [Feldman, 1968: 138].

Research supporting the notion of delinquent subcultures has a long history. The early research of Shaw and McKay

(1942) in Chicago, for example, described how in high delinquency areas of the city boys learned delinquent activities
from others and then initiated other boys into the activities.
While the social characteristics of the population might change,
the rates of delinquency in the areas tended to remain relatively constant.

The concept of delinquent subculture may help to explain
why lower-class urban slum areas tend to have high rates
of delinquency while the socioeconomic status of the youth
appears to be unrelated to delinquent behavior. As Johnson
(1979: 14-15) concludes: "The socioeconomic status of an
adolescent appears to be relatively unimportant, yet the class
of his or her nieghborhood—especially if it happens to be
a large lower-class sector—seems to play a role in generating
at least gang-type delinquency." Perhaps it is in such areas
that subcultures conducive to delinquent activities develop.
Once the subculture develops in a relatively homogeneous
lower class area, whoever lives in that neighborhood, regardless
of social class membership, would be expected to conform
to norms that endorse delinquent activity. In such an area,
there would be fewer controls to prevent individuals from
acting out the motivation to commit deviant acts. Further,
there would be more role models available by which such
acts could be learned. Finally, the opportunities for performing the acts would be increased. The failure to observe social
class differences and the performance of acts within that
area could be accounted for by the absence of social controls
that would ordinarily be operative for the middle-class youths
living in the area and by the greater circumstantial provoca-
tion for such acts. The greater opportunities and situational
requirements for the performance of the acts among the middle
class would be stronger influences on delinquency that would
be the potential controls exercised by inner restraints that
are not continually reinforced. Consistent with this reasoning,
Clark and Wenninger, although they did not find significant
differences in illegal behavior rates among social classes of

rural and small ruban areas, found that lower-class areas have higher illegal behavior rates, particularly regarding the more serious kinds of offenses. But within the areas, the socioeconomic classes did not differ with regard to delinquency. These investigators speculate on the basis of the findings, "that there are community-wide norms which are related to illegal behavior and to which juveniles adhere regardless of their social class origins" (Clark and Wenninger, 1962: 183).

ORIGIN AND PERSISTENCE OF DELINQUENT SUBCULTURES

The question of how delinquent subcultures originate and persist is dealt with at different points in this book in other connections and will be addressed only briefly here.

Answers to the question of how delinquent subcultures originate concern the related concepts of cultural diversity and political control, on the one hand, and collective motives and differential association, on the other. Answers to the question of how delinquent subcultures persist involve the related concepts of cultural transmission and social control.

Cultural Diversity and Political Control

In the former case, whether because of different cultural sources of immigrants or different rates of social change among segments of the population, diverse value systems develop. Differential political power permits the more influential segments of the population to legally define the behavior systems of other segments as illicit. The legal definition notwithstanding, the less powerful segments of the population continue to endorse and conform to the cultural patterns that are part of their tradition. The conformity by youths to subcultural patterns, some of which are defined as illegal, reflects a delinquent subculture.

Collective Motives and Differential Association

Individuals who are raised in a common cultural milieu accept the social demands made upon them as appropriate. The ability to meet those expectations is the measure of their feelings of self-worth. The failure to meet these expectations creates the need in those youths to behave in ways that will permit them to achieve these expectations or, failing that, to reduce the feelings of self-rejection that are associated with the failure. Those individuals, who have similar life experiences that preclude their achieving what they feel they should, develop similar needs, again, either to meet the demands made upon them or to reduce the feelings of self-rejection that result from the failure to do so. Through social interaction, facilitated by spatial proximity and similar social characteristics, they devise collective ways of adapting to their circumstances. As noted in Chapter 3, these collective solutions might involve the use of illegal means to achieve legitimate goals, attacks upon the validity of the normative standard or withdrawal from the normative standard by which the youths were judged to have failed to meet the demands made upon them, or the adoption of new standards that are more easily achieved simply by performing certain delinquent acts.

Cultural Transmission and Social Control

Once the youths have devised collective response patterns to their collective needs (those that permit them to meet the legitimate demands made upon them or to reduce any consequent feelings of self-rejection deriving from the failure to do so), the collective adaptive responses tend to have a life of their own. The collective adaptations have the force of morality. The rules are the right ways of behaving, and conformity to the rules is rewarded while deviation from the rules is punished in terms that are valued or disvalued by the group members. If the members of the group ever recognized the origins of the collective responses, they have long since forgotten them. New members who are attracted to the group learn what it takes to be accepted and otherwise rewarded by the group. They adopt the patterns and help pass them on to still other new members of the groups. The values attached to the behaviors and the goals of the groups are now independent of any value they may once have had and may continue to have in resolving the original needs of the collectivity that gave birth to the subculture.

In like manner, where the delinquent subculture was derived from cultural diversity, the ethnic traditions are transmitted from generation to generation, and deviation from subculturally approved patterns (including those that are defined as delinquent by the more inclusive society) are met with informally administered negative sanctions.

SUBCULTURAL AFFILIATION

Having asked and answered briefly how delinquent subcultures arise and persist, the question remains to be answered as to how the individual youth becomes affiliated with the delinquent subculture. Here the answers parallel those given in response to the question of deviant subcultures. The subcultures represents to the youth either cultural patterns that are to be conformed to by force of tradition or deviant attempts to satisfy needs that could not be satisfied through more conventional patterns.

Socialization and Delinquent Subcultures

A person may be born into and reared in a group that views formally defined delinquent patterns as compatible with traditional group values. The youth is socialized to recognize the appropriateness of these responses and motivated to behave accordingly in order to continue to evoke rewarding responses from group members. If any incongruity is noted between the group definition of the behavior as appropriate and the formal legal definition of the behavior as delinquent, then group justifications are provided that neutralize the perceived discrepancy.

The youths are exposed on a day to day basis to people who serve as a membership and positive reference group and who endorse the delinquent patterns. The youth's every-day satisfactions are dependent on people who appear by their behavior to endorse these patterns and he learns to model himself after these same people who offer the youth a range of satisfactions. Indeed, alternatives to the illicit patterns are not necessarily psychologically available to the youth. He may not even *conceive* of alternative response patterns.

Delinquent Subcultures as Deviant Satisfactions

An alternative route to the adoption of delinquent sub-cultures is provided by circumstances in which a youth who is reared in more conventional groups becomes attracted to and a member of a group that defines delinquent behaviors as appropriate. The attractiveness of the group is due to the youth's anticipation that important needs will be satisfied by the adoption of the subculture. The satisfactions may be directly tied to the delinquent patterns endorsed by the group. The delinquent behavior (for example, vandalism) or the fact of affiliation with a subculture that endorses the delinquent acts may serve to express the person's contempt for conventional standards by the measure of which the person must necessarily judge himself or herself a failure. By rejecting the standards, the youth feels it unnecessary to continue to feel unworthy.

Alternatively, the performance of the delinquent act may be incidental to the gratifications achieved from adoption of the delinquent subculture. The satisfactions may relate merely to being accepted by the group that endorses the delinquent act. Conforming to the subcultural norms represent ways of earning group approval. That some of the norms require illegal behavior is incidental to the group approval that is earned. In fact for the group itself, the illegal behavior may only be incidental to the fulfillment of other group values.

In any case whether the person is attracted to the group because of intrinsically satisfying delinquent behaviors or because of the potential satisfactions to be gained from acceptance by the group, the youth is motivated to remain a part of the group. A prerequisite for acceptance to the group is the conformity to group norms including those that endorse delinquent acts. Over time, however, because of the initial association in the youth's mind between the satisfactions to be gained from membership in the group and the delinquent patterns that are endorsed by the group, the youth comes to view the delinquent patterns and other group norms as attractive in their own right. The youth has become disposed to perform delinquent acts as appropriate responses by virtue of being a member of the group that shares the delinquent subculture.

SUMMARY

The motivation to commit delinquent acts is explained in part by the youth sharing with others a delinquent subculture. A delinquent subculture is a set of normative expectations shared by segments of a more inclusive population that include endorsements of behaviors that are legally defined as delinquent (whether or not the normative expectations also include prescriptions for nondelinquent behaviors). In some delinquent subcultures, such as the subculture of the professional thief, the delinquent activities are closely bound up with other aspects of group life including language, interpersonal life, and general style of living. In other delinquent subcultures, including many youth gangs, delinquent activities reflect a minor portion of the more inclusive set of norms that govern the youth's activities. In fact, the activity itself may have no intrinsic value except as it reflects some basic value that could be illustrated as well by nondelinquent activities.

The origin of delinquent subcultures may be accounted for by the cultural diversity of groups living in the same society. The people who share a delinquent subculture continue to endorse traditional values and activities although these may have been defined as illegal by more politically influential groups. Alternatively, subcultures may develop as a collective solution to the failure to achieve conventional goals through conventional means. Individuals who share the circumstances that lead to failure as well as the fact of failure in the course of social interaction adapt to their situation by coming to accept shared values that endorse the use of illicit activities (a) to achieve conventional goals, (b) as attacks upon conventional values, (c) to permit withdrawal from conventional society, or (d) as substitute standards for the measure of self-worth. These solutions either permit the achievement of values or reduce the feelings of self-rejection associated with the failure to achieve them.

Regardless of the source of the delinquent subculture, its persistence depends upon the transmission of the normative expectations to those who do not yet share the subcultural standards and the appropriate sanctioning of responses by those who share the subculture depending upon whether the responses conform to or deviate from the cultural standards (including those that endorse responses that are defined as delinquent activities).

The individual internalizes the culture by either being born into and reared in a group that shares a delinquent subculture or by later becoming attracted to such a group and becoming emotionally committed to the subcultural standards shared by the group. The person may become attracted to the group originally because of the delinquent activities that promise gratification to the youth and become committed to the group because of these gratifications. Alternatively, the youth may become attracted to the group independent of the delinquent activities but adopt the delinquent subculture as a means of evoking continued identification with the group the approval of which the youth needs. In any case, over time the youth learns to conform to the delinquent norms because such conformity is the conventional, right, fitting, or proper way to behave in the group that shares the delinquent subculture.

DISCUSSION QUESTIONS

1. What kinds of delinquent activities are explainable as reflections of ethnic differences in the population?

2. Think of the university as a society and the formal university rules as laws of the society. Describe how delinquent subcultures might develop as ways of adapting to failure to achieve university endorsed values by a) using illicit means to achieve legitimate goals or b) by reducing the feelings of self-rejection that accompany failure.

3. What are the processes by which delinquent patterns are transmitted to those who do not yet share the delinquent subculture?

5

ACTING OUT
DELINQUENT DISPOSITIONS

In the last two chapters it was observed that people may become motivated to perform delinquent acts because the youths anticipate that these behaviors will satisfy their needs. In conventional groups the delinquent behaviors may promise to meet needs to achieve conventional values (through illicit means) or to reduce the feelings of self-rejection that derive from the failure of the youths to achieve the conventional values. In groups that share delinquent subcultures, the delinquent behaviors may promise to meet the youths' needs to gain the approval of group members and other rewards associated with such approval, to behave in ways that are consistent with personal values, or to identify with a positively valued reference group.

The motivation to perform delinquent acts is part of the explanation for why people commit delinquent acts. Youths are more likely to commit delinquent acts if they are motivated to do so than if they are not motivated to do so. However, the motivation to perform delinquent behavior is only *part* of the explanation. Not all youths who are disposed or motivated to behave in certain ways, in particular, in ways that are contrary to the legal norms that are applicable, in fact perform those behaviors. This means that other factors are at work which prevent them from behaving in ways that they are disposed to.

Such factors might include the absence of opportunities to act out deviant dispositions. A youth may be disposed to use drugs but discover that none are available, or he or she may find that opportunities for breaking and entering are limited. Other factors include the expectations that satisfaction of more important needs will be satisfied by not performing the delinquent acts or that more important goals will be frustrated if the youth performs the deviant behaviors. Even a person who has the opportunity and the motivation to perform the delinquent behavior still might not act out the motive because he might be apprehended and punished, because the act was dangerous to his health, because those he cares about would disapprove, or simply because the youth believed the act was wrong. In short, the person who has the motivation and opportunity to commit a delinquent act still might not commit the act because of counteracting motives.

In the following pages, I will consider in some detail the nature of factors that constrain a youth from acting out deviant motivations. Whether or not a person acts out the disposition to commit delinquent acts will be viewed as depending upon (1) the strength of the motives to commit the act compared to the strength of the motives that dispose a person not to perform the act and (2) the situational context and other opportunities to perform the act.

Much of the sociological literature that relates to the question of why youths who are motivated to perform delinquent behavior do not do so has been classified as control theory (for example, Briar and Piliavin, 1965; Hewitt, 1970; Hirschi, 1969; Nye, 1958; Polk and Halferty, 1966). Rather than present the individual treatments of these theories, however, their elements will be considered in connection with the discussion of the variety of counteracting motives and opportunities that prevent a youth from acting out deviant dispositions. The counteracting motives and the opportunities for delinquent responses will be considered in turn.

COUNTERACTING MOTIVES

In earlier chapters it became clear that satisfaction of certain of the youth's needs may appear to the youth to depend upon the performance of delinquent acts, and so the youth is motivated to perform delinquent acts. In this chapter it should become equally clear that the satisfaction of other of the youths needs may appear to the youth to depend upon *not* performing delinquent acts. The projected delinquent behavior poses a threat to the satisfaction of important needs, and so the person is motivated to refrain from performing the delinquent behavior. If the satisfaction of the needs that appear to be threatened by the performance of delinquent behavior is more important to the youth than the satisfaction of the needs that is expected to result from the delinquent behavior, then the youth is likely to refrain from the delinquent behavior.

As will be noted below in greater detail, certain of the youth's needs are threatened just because the act is performed. The need to obey the law, to do what the youth's parents and friends think is right, or to be a moral person are examples of needs that would be threatened by the performance of delinquent behaviors and would be satisfied by refraining from delinquent acts. Other needs will be threatened because of expected *consequences* of the act itself. The need for the rewards granted by group members to the youth might be jeopardized if the youth was known to have performed delinquent acts or the need to be in control of one's own emotions might be threatened by the use of psychoactive substances. The threats posed to the satisfaction of such needs, then, influence the likelihood of acting out delinquent dispositions. This being the case, if the processes by which the person is restrained from delinquent behavior are to be understood, it is important to understand the origin of the needs that motivate the youth to restrain himself or herself from acting out impulses to perform delinquent acts.

Origin of Counteracting Motives

The process by which a person comes to develop motivation to conform to the normative expectations of society—that is, the way the youth comes to need, for example, positive responses from parents, success in school, and (later) occupational success—is a complex one. The way the youth develops a commitment to the conventions of society is based upon the infant's prolonged dependence upon other human beings for the satisfaction of his biological needs. Since the infant's needs are satisfied by the adults in the child's immediate social circle, he or she comes to value the presence of adults. However, as the circle of people in the child's world widens, the child may note that need satisfaction is associated with certain persons and not others. By a process of association, the child comes to value those people, and less directly the traits and behaviors associated with those people, who satisfy his needs. Conversely, the child comes to disvalue the traits and behaviors that are associated in the child's mind with those persons who frustrate the satisfaction of his or her biologically given or acquired values.

A particularly important set of behaviors and attributes associated with people who ordinarily satisfy our needs are those traits and behaviors that are apparent on the particular occasions when those people satisfy our needs. A mother ordinarily is associated with satisfying the child's needs. However, there are occasions when she does not do so. Those behaviors and traits (smiles, soft words, and the like) that are associated with the occasions when the needs are satisfied come to the valued in their own right. That is, the individual is motivated to evoke those responses that the child will later come to think of as approving responses. Conversely, those attributes or behaviors that are associated with the occasions when people who ordinarily satisfy the child's needs frustrate the satisfaction of those needs come to be regarded as undesirable in their own right. That is, the child will be motivated to avoid such behaviors. Later, the child will come to think of such behaviors as disapproval. Thus, the youth learns to value the positive and disvalue the negative attitudinal responses of others and the forms in which the attitudes are expressed—physical punishment, disapproving words, failure to reciprocate expectations.

Since people will display approving or disapproving responses depending upon the youth's characteristics and behaviors, the child will come to associate certain traits and behaviors with approving responses and other of his or her traits and behaviors with disapproving responses. In this way the child will come to evaluate behaviors and attributes as intrinsically worthy or unworthy because of their original association with approving and disapproving responses respectively. Finally, having learned to value such traits and behaviors, the youth comes to value in their own right any behavior patterns, resources, or relationships that he or she perceives to be instrumental to the achievement of these valued states.

In this way, in the ordinary course of socialization, the youth becomes emotionally attached to particular kinds of social relationships, particular attributes and behaviors that are associated with valued others, and personal attributes, behaviors, or experiences. The person has come to need the presence and approving responses of adults who have particular kinds of characteristics and behave in particular ways and to possess the kinds of traits, to perform the kinds of behaviors, and to enjoy the kinds of experiences that are approved by these others. The satisfaction of these needs becomes the person's measure of self-worth. The youth is motivated to behave in ways that will reflect or be instrumental in the satisfaction of these needs and, thus, in ways that will evoke self-accepting attitudes. The person becomes emotionally invested in the image of self as one who has certain identities and conforms to the role expectations that are associated with those identities. If the social positions or identities are conventional ones and are defined in terms of conventional rules, then the person's self-conceptions will include images of self as not violating the law (Reckless et al., 1956).

The processes by which the youth (1) becomes emotionally attached to the network of relationships and the expectations of the people in those relationships regarding appropriate traits, behaviors, and experiences; and (2) comes to evaluate himself in terms of conventional standards have implications for both the development and the acting out of deviant dispositions. To the extent that the person becomes attracted to and evaluates himself in terms of conventional values, to that extent will he forego engaging in delinquent behaviors that threaten his needs to achieve those values. The extent to which the person evaluates himself in terms of conventional values, however, will be influenced by the degree to which the youth satisfies those needs by achieving conventional values. As was observed in Chapter 3, the consistent failure to achieve and to evaluate oneself positively according to conventional standards decreases the youth's emotional commitment to those standards and increases the likelihood that the youth will develop dispositions to engage in delinquent behaviors that promise to achieve conventional goals or to reduce the feelings of self-rejection that are the consequence of failure to do so.

Varieties of Counteracting Motives

Any of a number of motives may restrain a youth from committing a delinquent act that he or she is otherwise motivated to perform. The self-restraint might come from the anticipation that important needs might be satisfied by *not* performing the delinquent act. For example, the youths feels good about himself when he does the "right thing." The youth feels an ongoing need to be law abiding. This need is satisfied when the youth resists temptations to violate the law. Alternatively, the youth may be restrained from acting out delinquent impulses because the youth anticipates that the performance of the delinquent act will frustrate the satisfaction of important personal needs. The youth may have an ongoing need to be respected by others. He may anticipate that the satisfaction of this need (by being respected by others) will be frustrated if they find out he or she committed a delinquent act.

The youth's anticipation of the achievement or frustration of need satisfaction may be perceived by the youth as being more or less directly related to the nonperformance or performance of the act. The *direct* involvement of the delinquent act is perceived when the fact of not performing or of performing the delinquent act provides or frustrates need satisfaction. The youth satisfies his need to be a law-abiding person or frustrates his need to conform to the expectations of his family and friends by virtue of performing the delinquent act. *Less directly,* delinquent behavior is perceived by the youth as having consequences that reflect the satisfaction or frustration of the youth's needs. It is not the delinquent behavior itself but the consequences of the behavior that satisfies or frustrates strong needs. Thus, the youth may perceive that conformity to the law will have consequences (for example, a good job and other rewards associated with conformity) that satisfy needs and that delinquent behavior will have consequences (being rejected by loved ones, going to jail) that frustrate needs.

The anticipated satisfactions associated with the act or consequences of conformity and the anticipated frustrations associated with the act or consequences of delinquent behavior, to the extent that they outweigh the projected benefits of the delinquent behavior, will prevent the youth from acting out any delinquent dispositions the youth might experience. I consider the direct and indirect motivational implications of delinquent behavior in turn.

Direct Motivational Implications

The acts of conforming to certain legal norms and of failing to perform delinquent acts when tempted directly satisfy a number of needs; and the acts of violating legal norms immediately frustrate diverse needs. From among these many motives, I consider in some detail three general motives for conforming to legal norms and for refraining from performing delinquent acts: (1) because the behaviors prescribed by the law are morally right or the behaviors forbidden by the laws are morally wrong; (2) because the legally prescribed acts are appropriate or the legally forbidden acts are inappropriate for people characterized by specified social identities; (3) because the social network in which the youth is involved judges the legally prescribed behavior to be right or the legally proscribed behavior to be wrong.

Moral commitment. A youth is unlikely to perform a delinquent act if the youth believes that the act is a violation of a rule that is right. The person is emotionally committed to the rule which to him reflects valued behavior (doing what is right, not doing what is wrong). Many studies, in fact, are fairly consistent in showing a relationship between belief in the rightness of conventional norms and not engaging in delinquent acts (Siegal et al., 1973; Hindelang, 1974; Hepburn, 1976). For example, data from a survey of subjects in three states (Tittle, 1980) suggest the conclusion that counterbalancing motivations, stimulated by beliefs that certain acts are serious and immoral, reduce the likelihood of future performance of the act. Individuals who judge an act as wrong, as serious, and as requiring that a law be passed against such behavior are less likely to anticipate some likelihood of performing the act in the future compared to those people who judge that the act was not wrong, was not serious, and did not require laws being passed against it. For example, only 13 percent of those who judged that the act of assault was morally wrong, compared to 45 percent of those who judged that the act was not wrong, indicated that they might commit assault in the future; only 12 percent of those who judged assault to be serious, compared to 52 percent of those who judged the act not to be serious, indicated that they might commit assault in the future; and only 13 percent of those who indicated that a law against assault should be passed, compared with 28 percent who indicated that a law against assault should not be passed, suggested that they might perform the act in the future.

The performance of the delinquent act, however, does not necessarily preclude some moral commitment to the norm. It is possible to commit a delinquent act in the face of moral commitment to a rule that proscribes it under either or both of two circumstances. First, a person may be able to justify the act with reference to other higher order rules. Thus, Gresham Sykes and David Matza (1957) point out a number of "techniques of neutralization" by which the delinquent described circumstances that justify the violation of legal norms. Indeed, it is the apparent need to justify the violation that suggests there is some degree of commitment to the legal norms. Implicitly, the youths are saying that it is wrong to steal unless someone steals from him first or that it is wrong to beat someone up unless the victim first insulted the youth. Second, a person may be simultaneously committed to conflicting sets of rules, one of which sets reflects the legal norms of society. Frequently, the performance of a delinquent act need not imply the *total* absence of commitment to conventional norms or to the conventional groups that endorse those norms. Rather, it may reflect a *greater* commitment to a competing set of norms. As long as the person's commitment to conventional norms does not conflict with the commitment to the norms of another group, the person may simultaneously conform to both the conventional norms and the norms of the other group. However, where the norms of the other group preclude conformity to the norms of conventional society and, indeed, may require violation of conventional norms (as when acceptance by a counterculture group requires that the youth participate in destruction of public property), the greater commitment to counterculture norms may result in the performance of the delinquent act of vandalism. Nevertheless the simultaneous commitment to conventional makes the youth vulnerable to influences that would reduce the youth's involvement in illicit patterns of behavior.

Moral commitment is inextricably involved with other motives that restrain a youth from committing delinquent acts. One such set of motives to be considered presently is the youth's need to conform to the norms endorsed by the relational structure in which the youth is involved. The belief in the moral validity of conventional values may well be influenced by emotional ties that the individuals forms to significant others, particularly, the emotional attachment to family and school (Wiatrowski et al., 1981). Consistent with this conclusion, Johnson (1979) reported that positive attitudes expressed by parents to children and the resulting emotional attachment to the parents are related to positive attitudes toward other conventional values (such as school activities and achievements) that the parents may be presumed to support.

Role-inappropriate behavior. Moral commitment implies that the rule is universally applicable. Under whatever qualifications are stated, the norm applies to all regardless of social-identity or other personal characteristics. The person restrains himself from performing delinquent responses because it is morally right to do so and expects that others would be similarly motivated. However, certain legally and morally binding rules, in addition to or instead of being morally binding on all members of society are particularly applicable to what is considered the proper behavior of segments of the population who are characterized by particular social identities.

As the youth matures, the satisfaction of his needs depends upon the responses of other group members. How the group responds to the youth depends upon whether or not the youth possesses the attributes that are valued by the group and performs the behaviors that are expected of him. The particular attributes that the youth is expected to have and the behaviors he is expected to perform depends upon the social identities that he has. If the youth displays the attributes and behaviors that are appropriate ot his various social identities (particularly to those identities that are considered most important), the group will respond in ways that satisfy the youth's needs (for example, the need for approval) or that permit him to gain satisfaction of his needs (providing him with instrumental resources such as money, property, influence). Over time, the youth's association of his social identities and of attributes and behaviors that fulfill those identities on the one hand with the need-satisfying responses from group members on the other hand lead to the positive intrinsic valuation of his social identities and of the attributes and behaviors that are required of people with those identities. The youth needs to think of himself or herself in terms of certain identities and in terms of the attributes and behaviors associated with those identities.

As this applies to self-restraint against acting out delinquent dispositions, if the delinquent act is perceived as being contrary to the proper behavior associated with a valued identity, the person will be motivated to forego the expected satisfactions of the delinquent act in favor of the more role-appropriate behavior that proscribed such acts. For example, a woman might restrain herself from committing an illegal violent act not only because it is illegal or because of any consequences that might occur if she was apprehended but also because she is a woman, and deviant acts, in general, and violent acts, in particular, are unwomanly, that is, inappropriate for women to do. If particular delinquent acts violate the normative expectations associated with social identities that are important to the person, then they will restrain themselves from committing those acts even if the opportunity and motivation to commit the act are present. Both those who share the identity and those who do not agree that the performance of certain kinds of acts are inappropriate for those who share the identity. They may agree that the performance of the act is inappropriate because people with that identity (people in that social position or status) do not commit illegal acts in general or do not commit acts (that may happen to be illegal) that otherwise violate the role expectations that apply to people who have that identity.

A number of research projects have reported findings that are consistent with the argument that women are more motivated to refrain from particular kinds of delinquent acts and, indeed, from delinquent acts in general. Consistent with the thesis that the disposition to deviant activity is a violation of normal sex role-related adaptive patterns is the observation, particularly in self-report studies, of a high male/female sex ratio for offenses involving force and violence (Hindelang et al., 1981). Such studies (whether they use official statistics or self-report data) generally agree that males are more likely than females to commit offenses, particularly serious offenses (Hindelang et al., 1981; Tittle, 1980). Tittle, using survey data collected in three states, not only reported that males were proportionately more likely than females to have reported thefts, marijuana smoking, illegal gambling, and assault, but were also more likely than females to project some possibilities of future performance of such acts. The fact that the differences between the sexes are far less among those who grew up in households without a father and where the female was equal to or greater in independence than the male suggests that role modeling may be part of the explanation for the gender-related differences. This is consistent with conjectures about the socialization process for males and females that have frequently been offered.

Females have traditionally been identified with conforming roles, moral restraints, and more conservative life patterns. Pressures and social demands dictate that women are to be compliant, obedient, dependent and moral. . . , and the training experiences of early life tend to be less conducive to deviant behavior among females [Tittle, 1980: 81].

The presence of an independent male head of household as a condition for observing greater conformity on the part of females is congruent with the reasoning that the female spouse would be better able to conform to traditional female role expectations and, thereby, serve as a conforming role model for the female children. The male/female differential in delinquent offenses appears to be independent of race, marital status, age, religious preference, socioeconomic status, place of residence, and family background.

These data suggest that the socialization process, in the course of which the person becomes committed to certain social identities, in some degree influences the individual not to act out deviant dispositions that are inappropriate to those social identities.

Commitment to social relationships. A youth is less likely to commit a delinquent act even if the youth does not believe the rule that the act violates is important and even if the act is not inappropriate to the youth's salient social identities if the person is emotionally attached to groups or social systems that endorse the rule. If the person very much cares what his parents think and they believe that it is important to conform to the rule, the youth will do so even if he does not think there is really anything wrong with violating the particular rule. More abstractly, a youth may become emotionally attached to the more inclusive society, including its legal institutions. The youth will respect and will tend not to violate the law even if he does not believe in the particular law (and even if the opportunity to perform the delinquent act is present, he believes he will derive pleasure from the act, and he does not believe he will be punished or otherwise suffer adverse consequences).

The distinction is drawn between a person's emotional commitment to a rule and the individual's involvement in a system of social relationships. Both variables reflect influences that may deter an individual from committing a delinquent act even though the youth is otherwise motivated to perform the act. The emotional commitment to the norm prevents the individual from performing the act because he believes that the rule is right and to perform the delinquent act would be a violation of the rule (that is, morally wrong). Involvement in a system of social relationships, however, inhibits the expression of deviant impulses regardless of the person's emotional commitment to the norm. Here, the individual does not act out a deviant impulse because those with whom he is involved in a network or social relationships believe it is wrong. To draw a distinction between the two kinds of commitment, however, is not to say that they are unrelated. Indeed, over time the person's belief in the rightness of the rules will increase as he perceives that they are accepted as right by the people he is attracted to; and the youth will be increasingly emotionally attached to the conventional groups as they reward his behavior as conforming to the rules that they endorse.

Research findings tend to support the view that people are less likely to act out delinquent dispositions under conditions that suggest involvement in a range of social relationships. Conversely, under conditions that weaken emotional attachments to others, deviant behavior is more likely to be observed. Consistent with the idea that individuals who are fully integrated into a network of conventional social relationships would be less likely to commit delinquent acts, Tittle (1980) reports findings that indicate that independent of other explanatory factors, a measure of involvement in conventional social relationships was inversely related to the person's estimates of some probability of performing specified illegal acts (theft, marijuana smoking, illegal gambling, assault) in the future. Involvement in conventional social relationships (social integration) was measured in terms of such items as the number of people in the immediate neighborhood the respondent knew personally and the amount of interest the respondent said most people in the community had in how people like the respondent acted. People with higher scores on the measure of social integration were less likely to indicate some probability of performing the deviant acts in the future. Further, people whose community was described as relatively high in community spirit were less likely to have reported theft and marijuana smoking during the past five years than people whose communities were described as relatively low in community spirit. These relationships remain stable when age, sex, geographic mobility, and size of place are controlled. Finally, people who reported higher levels of religious participation relative to those who reported lower levels were generally less likely to report having performed specified illegal acts during the past five years and were less likely to report some probability of future performance of such acts. This relationship held even after controlling on religion, age, gender, race, and size of place of residence.

Regarding the influence of weakened social relationships, Tittle (1980) reports data that are consistent with the idea that the weakening of social ties to members of the community increases the likelihood that people will not feel constrained to inhibit any deviant motives they experience. One of the experiences that people have that might reduce their ties to others is geographic mobility. Tittle found that particularly among younger people, there is a positive relationship between geographic mobility (number of counties lived in within the past ten years) and both deviant acts committed within the past five years and projected probability of future deviant acts. The data are consistent with the belief that people who move around a lot are less likely to develop strong relationships with people and, therefore, are less likely to prevent themselves from performing deviant acts that they might otherwise want to perform because these people disapprove of such acts.

More directly, data from cross-sectional studies are consistent in reporting that rejecting attitudes by parents (Hindelang, 1973; Hirschi, 1969) and failure in school (Elliott and Voss,

1974; Gibbons, 1976) are associated with higher level of delinquency. Data from a longitudinal study of junior high school
students in Houston (Kaplan et al., 1984) also are consistent
with the hypothesis that the weakening of emotional ties
with conventional groups permits youths who are so motivated
to actually perform delinquent acts. Individuals who in the
seventh grade reported feelings of rejection by and failure
in conventional groups (family and school) were more likely
in the eighth grade to report having performed deviant acts
(after controlling for the performance of deviant acts and
other variables in the seventh grade). Presumably, the experience of negative consequences in the social groups led
to a reduction in the value attached to the attitudes of people
in those groups. Therefore, if the youth were motivated to
perform delinquent acts, they would not feel inhibited from
doing so because of the attitudes of people in the groups
from which they had emotionally withdrawn.

Indirect Motivational Implications

The earlier discussion has argued that among the motives
that lead a youth to refrain from committing delinquent acts
(although the act might satisfy certain of the youth's needs)
are the need to perform moral acts, the need to perform
role-appropriate behavior, and the need to do what the people
with whom the youth interacts in the context of social relationships think the youth should do. The youth is motivated
to refrain from committing a delinquent act in order to satisfy
these needs or to avoid the threat to the satisfaction of these
needs that the delinquent behaviors represent. The motivational significance of the delinquent behavior is in the immediate performance of the act.

However, the youth may also refrain from performing
a delinquent act because of the motivational significance of
the *consequences* of the act rather than of the act itself.
Among the reasons that he does not perform the delinquent

behavior is because he thinks he might be caught and punished or because the act was too dangerous to his health. These are particularly important influences on preventing the behavior when the youth does not believe that the law he is thinking about breaking is right. Many times a person will obey a rule not because it is believed to be right to do so (think about obeying the speed limit as a case in point) but because of what bad things might happen to him if the rule is not obeyed (he might get a ticket or get involved in an accident). Were it not for these possibilities, the person might well violate the law by speeding in order to get where he is going sooner, to enjoy the thrill of going fast, or for some other gratifying reason.

The youth who is raised in a particular society has adopted the values of that society. When the youth sees the achievement of what is valued as tied to conformity to the rules of society and views the performance of delinquent acts as threats to present and future rewards, the youth will be motivated to conform to the rules and to resist acting upon any dispositions and opportunity to perform delinquent acts. If the youth is motivated to achieve future social success and views being labelled as a delinquent as a threat to such success, the youth will be disposed to refrain from performing the delinquent act.

Whether or not a person is deterred from performing delinquent acts that he is otherwise motivated to perform by the expectation of certain consequences depends upon how much the person values (or disvalues) the outcomes in question. If the person believes that, as consequences of performing a delinquent act, he or she will lose the respect of loved ones, personal freedom, and the opportunity to achieve other valued ends in the future, then there is reason to believe that the youth will be deterred from performing the act. However, if the person does not think about these outcomes, of if the youth thinks about these outcomes but regards them as very unlikely occurrences, and/or doesn't think these outcomes are very important, then there is little reason to believe that the individual motivated to perform the delinquent act will (given the opportunity) fail to do so.

In the limited space available, it is not possible to consider the motivational significance of all of the consequences of refraining from or of engaging in delinquent behavior. Therefore, in a general way the motivational significance of only two classes of consequences of delinquent behavior will be considered. The first class of consequences relates to informal sanctions, including changes in the attitudes and behaviors of those with whom the person interacts in the context of social relationships. The attitudes and behaviors of others that might be evoked by the youth's delinquency could be motivationally significant in themselves or insofar as they are related to the perceived satisfaction or frustration of other of the youth's needs. The second class of consequences relates to formal sanctions, including arrest and incarceration. Again, these outcomes might be motivationally significant in themselves or because of their perceived effects on the satisfaction or frustration of other of the youth's needs.

Informal sanctions. The network of relationships in which the youth is involved is intrinsically valued and is instrumental to the achievement of any of a number of other rewards. In fact, the positive valuation of the social relationships is traceable to the instrumental role played by the others to whom the youth relates with regard to the satisfaction of the youth's needs. To violate the expectations of others by committing delinquent acts would be to risk the stability of the relationships that the youth values and the rewards that are instrumental to the achievement of other valued goals.

Research findings are consistent with this conclusion. Tittle (1980), for example, reported data that suggest a relationship between fear of negative sanctions and the person's estimate that he would perform deviant acts in the future. Whether fear of sanctions was measured by a more general scale or by the person's perception of potential loss of respect from persons known personally if caught doing the deviant act, individuals with greater fear of sanctions were less likely to report some probability of performing acts of theft, marijuana smoking, illegal gambling, and assault in the future. These results are particularly significant since these relationships were observed after controlling for a large number of other theoretically significant explanations of deviant behavior including degree of moral commitment, differential association, social integration, and past contact with the authorities.

In fact, when fear of negative sanctions is measured as the perception of loss of respect from significant others if caught doing the deviant act, fear of sanctions appears to be generally the most important predictor of projected future performance of the deviant act. Among the illegal acts of a theft of $5, theft of $50, smoking marijuana, illegal gambling, and assault, only in the case of marijuana smoking was fear of interpersonal respect loss not the most important predictor of projected future performance of the act (and in that instance it was still a significant predictor, although third in importance). Relative to other theoretical variables, then, fear of sanctions is a potent predictor of estimates of future performance of deviant acts. Tittle goes on to point out, however, that even when considering the explanatory value of all of the variables together, much of the variance in deviant behavior remains to be explained.

Formal sanctions. There exists some uncertainty about whether or not and the conditions under which arrest, adjudication, and its consequences influence delinquent behavior (Zimring and Hawkins, 1973; Palmer, 1977; Johnson, 1979; Tittle, 1980). There are a number of studies that indicate that where punishment is more severe and there is greater certainty that the punishment will in fact be administered, there are fewer crimes committed. Some of the studies measure the actual probabilities of arrest and administration of sanctions of varying degrees of severity. Other studies look at how the youths *perceive* the likelihood of being caught and being the object of more or less severe punishments. It is important to make this distinction since what the youth *believes* is the true state of affairs is most likely to have direct effects on his behavior. If the youth *believes* that he would be caught and punished severely if he performed the act, he might not act even though in fact the chances are slim that he would be caught and (if caught) receive a severe sentence.

In fact, a large number of delinquent acts go undetected and unpunished. Conversely, if a youth believed that the chances were slim that he would be caught and punished severely if he performed a delinquent act, he might act even if in reality there was a good chance that he would be caught and punished. One of the influences upon what a person believes is the reality of the situation. A youth is more likely to believe that there *is* a good chance of being caught if in fact there *is* a good chance of the event being detected, judged, and punished severely.

However, the relationship is an imperfect one. Many youths believe that the certainty and severity of punishment is greater or lesser than it actually is. Those youths who are more likely to correctly perceive the chances of being apprehended and more or less severely punished are more likely to be those who are intimately involved with delinquent associates and personal delinquent experiences. Since almost all delinquent acts go undetected, the more the adolescent associates with those who have committed delinquent acts, the more likely the youth is to be aware of how relatively little risk there is in the delinquent act. In addition, the presence of a group may reduce the felt risk by creating a safety-in-numbers feeling for the youth contemplating delinquency. On the other hand, incorrect perceptions of risk may be the consequence of emotional attachment to adult authority figures. Among the conventional values that are passed on by parents to whom the peer becomes emotionally attached is the belief that there is a high risk of apprehension for delinquency. Johnson noted such an association and interpreted it as possibly indicating, "that adolescents more attached to their parents are more likely to believe conventional maxims that parents tend to espouse, including crime doesn't pay, in spite of (or in ignorance of) contradictory evidence" (Johnson, 1979: 103).

Perhaps because of the different likelihoods of engaging in such relationships with delinquent peers and adult representatives of conventional society, as well as for other reasons, different segments of the population perceive different risks of formal sanctions for engaging in illicit acts. With regard to gender differences, for example, one of the explanations for why women appear to be less likely to commit delinquent acts is that females are more likely than males to believe that they would be arrested (as well as lose respect among personal acquaintances) if they committed any of several delinquent acts (Tittle, 1980). With regard to racial differences, nonwhites are more likely than whites to perceive relatively high chances of arrest for specified deviant acts.

In one study (Tittle, 1980) 35 percent of the whites, compared to 50 percent of the nonwhites, perceived a 50-50 or greater chance of arrest for a $5 theft. However, white subjects were more sensitive to the possibility of loss of interpersonal respect for committing delinquent acts, although both races in absolute terms estimated high chances of loss of interpersonal respect.

Finally, it is particularly interesting that perceived risk of formal sanctions for illegal behavior is related to socioeconomic status. Although people of lower socioeconomic status have not been consistently observed to commit more delinquent acts, nevertheless it is possible that motivation to deviance may be higher in these groups but fear of formal sanctions deters them from committing the acts to a much greater extent than the lesser motivated higher classes. Consistent with this reasoning, Tittle (1980) reported that lower socioeconomic status subjects are more likely to perceive a 50-50 or greater chance of arrest for specified deviant acts than people in higher socioeconomic status categories. For example, for marijuana smoking only 36 percent of the high socioeconomic status people perceive this probability of arrest compared with 49 percent of the middle status people and 54 percent of the low socioeconomic status people. For $50 theft, 58 percent of the high socioeconomic status people, 68 percent of the middle status people and 74 percent of the low socioeconomic status people perceive a 50-50 or greater chance of arrest for committing the act.

There is another influence upon perceived risk of formal sanction. Among males, particularly, the perception of the parent as not loving or being concerned about them makes the child susceptible to influence by peers, perhaps in an attempt to gain approval from another social source. The susceptibility to peer influences increases the perceived risks of being apprehended for delinquent acts which in turn decreases the likelihood of the performance of delinquent behavior (Johnson, 1979). Perhaps the susceptibility to peer influence relfects the underlying timidity or fearfulness related to loss of self confidence as a result of being unloved by parents.

Regardless of the nature of the influences upon perceived risk of formal sanctions, however, studies of both subjective and objective certainty and severity of punishment have reported that higher risk of punishments or severity of punishment is associated with lower rates of delinquency (although studies are also available that find no such relationships). Gibbs (1968) found that states with higher certainty of punishment (measured by the ratio of the state's prison admissions for murder in 1960 to the average number of known murders in 1959 and 1960) and greater severtity of punishment (measured in terms of median number of months served by the state's homicide inmates as of December 1960) tended to have lower homicide rates. Bean and Cushing (1971) reported that even after the effect of region was taken into account, certainty and severity of punishment still had an inverse effect on homicide rates.

Other studies also suggest conditions that visibly increase the risk of being apprehended decrease the likelihood of acting out delinquent impulses. Skogan and Maxfield (1981) refer to data that are compatible with the view that such protective measures as watchdogs, alarms, and lights deter incidents of housebreaking, although they also point out that other interpretations of the data are possible.

Experiments indicate that when the adoption of household protective measures is widespread in a target neighborhood, victimization rates drop there relative to other, control neighborhoods. The evidence on whether this constitutes true crime prevention, or if crime simply is displaced into other cateogories or into other neighborhoods, is not persuasive one way or the other [Skogan and Maxfield, 1981: 264].

The extent to which threats of formal sanctions deter a person contemplating future violations of the law may depend upon *threshold* of severity or certainty of sanction. A particular *level* of severity or certainty of formal (or informal) sanctions may have to be perceived before the perception has a deterrent effect. As Tittle summarizes his findings, it appears that

in general an informal sanction threat has to be perceived to be quite certain before there is a deterrent effect attributable to that perception and a legal threat has to be perceived as very severe before there is a deterrent effect attributable to that perception. On the other hand, an informal threat may be perceived as moderately severe and still deter whereas a legal threat may be perceived as only mdoerately certain and still deter [1980: 322].

Although fear of different kinds of legal sanctions (arrest, going to jail) have some deterrent effect on certain kinds of illegal acts, there exists some question as to how strong and direct the effect of such fear is upon deviant behavior.

Regarding the relative strength of the effect, Tittle reports that perceived informal sanctions (loss of interpersonal respect, discovery by acquaintances, estimate of the amount of community respect loss that would result from discovery of deviance, and so on) are far more effective than formal ones in inhibiting the expression of deviant acts among individuals who are otherwise motivated to perform illegal acts. Regarding the directness of the effect, data from the same study suggest that although controlling for formal sanctions has no effect on the predictive power of informal sanctions, the reverse is not the case. When informal sanctions are controlled, formal sanctions appear not to be predictive of inhibition of deviant dispositions. Tittle concludes that formal sanctions produce a deterrent effect only insofar as they influence the perceived likelihood of informal sanctions that then inhibit deviant behavior.

Nevertheless, while the effects of perceived formal sanctions is slight (relative to the effect of informal sanctions) and indirect, it may have an appreciable effect in absolute terms since perception of legal sanctions influence that segment of the population that is inclined to perform deviant acts, that is those who have already committed deviant acts and those who are highly motivated to commit serious deviant acts.

> There is a noticeable pattern suggesting that those who have been arrested are more deterred by their perceptions of sanctions then those who have not been arrested. And because potential violators of the law are probably disproportionately represented by individuals who have a desire to commit legal violations, who have committed them before, and who have been arrested for legal offenses, even the marginal deterrence suggested here for those people could have a noticeable effect on the crime rate [Tittle, 1980: 321-322].

Whether or not the threat of consequences of an anticipated delinquent act prevents the occurrence of the act by the youth who is motivated to perform a delinquent act, the existence of punitive responses to delinquent acts may serve other functions with regard to the prevention of delinquent behavior. When consequences that are culturally defined as bad are observed by youths to inevitably follow upon delinquent acts, the punishment comes to symbolize the immorality of the act, and in time the youth comes to think of the act as immoral. This process may take place even if the youths themselves never contemplated the performance of the act. The association in the youth's mind of the punishment with the act leads to the intrinsic disevaluation of the delinquent act. Even in the absence of the cues of punishment, the act is regarded as "bad,"

Johnson (1979: 32) points to still other mechanisms by which punishment might forestall delinquent acts.

> Threats may also initiate conforming behavior that later becomes habit. The threatened punishment may be forgotten or even removed, whereas the behavior continues. Finally, under many conditions adolescents feel pressures (from peers or unusual situational factors) to break a law, while still feeling wrong about doing so. In these cases the fact of the existence of threatened punishment may be called forth to provide an excuse or rationale for conformity.

Moderating Factors

The relationship between fear of formal or informal sanctions and the acting out of delinquent dispositions is not a simple one. The nature of the relationship is moderated by a number of factors. For example, Johnson (1979) observed higher perceived risk of apprehension to be associated with less delinquent behavior among white males, but perceived risk was unrelated to delinquency among white females. Perhaps white males perceived an association between apprehension and threat to other personal values (for example, occupational success), while females did not perceive such an association. However, race and gender might reflect differences in any of a number of other influences as well.

In like manner the deterrent effect of different sanctions appears to be related to the kind of illegal acts under consideration (Tittle, 1980). The person's estimate of the probability of being arrested and jailed for performing the act appears to have greater deterrent effects on illegal gambling and assault compared to the effect on deterring theft or marijuana smoking. The person's estimate of the probability of being discovered by anyone who might disapprove is a more effective deterrent for theft than for marijuana smoking, illegal gambling, or assault. The person's estimate of the probability of exposure to the community as a whole is relatively effective in deterring marijuana smoking compared to the other illegal acts. The person's estimate of the amount of interpersonal respect that would be lost if caught is more effective in deterring illegal gambling, small theft, and assault than large theft and marijuana smoking.

The literature suggests two general conditions that might account for a large number of instances in which specific variables were observed to moderate the relationship between the fear of formal or informal sanctions and the performance of delinquent acts. These conditions relate to emotional attraction to the conventional order and to the ability to define the delinquent act as compatible with the conventional order.

Attraction to the Conventional Order

For the youth to forego the performance of delinquent acts because he believes it is wrong, because people he relates to think it is wrong, because it is inappropriate to his social identities, or because it will evoke informal and formal responses by others, it is necessary that the youth be emotionally invested in the moral beliefs, social relationships and identities, and responses by others. If the youth did not *care* about these things, they would not influence his behavior. The effectiveness of counterbalancing motives that prevent a youth (who is motivated to commit a delinquent act and who has the opportunity to commit a delinquent act) from acting out his motivations to deviant behavior are tied up with his positive feelings about the conventional order. The youth is attracted to representatives of the conventional moral order and needs positive responses from them. Further, he respects the rightness of conventional rules and would feel guilty if he violated them. Finally, he gains gratifications from his participation in social relationships and would not like to risk the loss of present and anticipated future satisfactions that might be among the consequences of his performing deviant acts.

Whether over the short term or longer term, any of a number of factors might reduce the youth's emotional attraction to the conventional world. Over the short term, any factors that influence the person's emotional and cognitive states in general and awareness of the youth's conventional social identities in particular might reduce the effectiveness of constraints against acting out delinquent dispositions. The nature of some delinquent activities is such that they may reduce the constraints that might ordinarily (in the absence of these delinquent acts) prevent the acting out of *other* delinquent acts. Thus, for example, while under the influence of alcohol or other substances that affect emotional and cognitive states, the person might commit crimes against property or violent acts that might not be committed in more drug-free states. It seems reasonable to assume that substance abuse might reduce the subjective emotional significance of such deterrents as fear of punishment, feelings of guilt, and the emotional attachment of the youth to his parents. Other circumstances allow the youth to ignore his conventional social identities and, therefore, the emotional significance of conforming to the role expectations that define those identities. Such circumstances as being part of an anonymous crowd permit the youth to submerge his identities and, thus, the recognition that the delinquent acts he is motivated to perform violate the role expectations that under less anonymous circumstances he would be motivated to honor.

Over the longer term, the emotional attraction to the representatives, moral code, and activities of the moral order depend in part upon how successful the person was in achieving what he values within conventional society. The very same experiences of failure (such as feeling rejected by family, friends, or school and failing to attain other valued attributes such as getting good grades, being popular, or good looking) that make a person ready to seek satisfactions through delinquent acts influence the weakening of the youth's ties to the conventional system. If the person experiences failure and associates that failure with the conventional order, then he will become decreasingly attracted to the conventional society at the same time he is becoming attracted to the potential satisfactions of deviant behavior. In that event the deviant motivation will be more likely to have actual deviant behavior as an outcome.

Yet, common sense tells us that people who are disposed to perform delinquent acts frequently do refrain from performing such acts because of the above-mentioned reasons. This being the case, we must assume that the experiences of failure are rarely extreme enough to fully counteract the attachment to the social order that is associated with the youth's degree of experience with success. Although the strength of commitment to the social order may be weakened by failure, it still remains, in general, a potent force in forestalling the acting out of delinquent motivations. It is only in extreme circumstances of near total failure to achieve what is expected by conventional standards that the youth's attraction to the normative order ceases to restrain delinquent impulses. Short of such extreme circumstances, a number of the youth's satisfactions will continue to depend upon conventional norms, identities and relationships and the youth will tend to restrain delinquent impulses. As Richard E. Johnson (1979: 6), referring to the control theory perspective, puts it so succinctly: "A school failure has little to lose by being caught in a delinquent act; a school success risks losing both current rewarding experiences and future educational and occupational opportunities."

Conventional Justification

It is not enough that the youth be emotionally attracted to the conventional in order for deviant impulses to be restrained. A youth, attracted to the social order, might be motivated to do the right thing, to behave appropriately in various social capacities, to do what those with whom he interacts think is right, to elicit approving responses from others, to avoid social sanctions and still act out a deviant disposition. All that is necessary for this to occur is for the youth who is committed to the conventional moral order to justify performance of the act in terms that the youth thinks are consistent with the conventional moral code and are acceptable to the conventional groups to which he is attracted.

The youth may be able to justify illicit acts in terms of the standards that apply specifically for adolescents or in terms of standards that are more generally applied in society. Illegal activities may be justified in terms of doing it for kicks or because it is exciting or for other reasons that may be acceptable when applied to adolescent behavior. Other illicit activities such as violence are perhaps justifiable in terms of patterns that are endorsed informally in various social institutions. Violence in legitimated form is a prevalent pattern in recreational activities (television, sports) and global political strategy (war). Perhaps illegal violence is only an extension of acceptable patterns in unusual circumstances. If violence is so much a part of conventional life, it may be relatively easy to justify the behavior in spite of its illegality (although internalized respect for the law still might act as something of a constraint against the illegal activity).

Consistent with this observation, Johnson (1979) finds that having friends that commit delinquent acts is associated with self-justifications of delinquent behaviors, and self-justification of delinquent behaviors in turn is associated with performing delinquent acts.

In any case, for a person who indeed is motivated to gain the satisfactions that are reflected in or gained from conforming behavior, the illicit activity must be defined as acceptable when measured against conventional standards.

OPPORTUNITIES

The performance of delinquent behavior is influenced by the youth's earlier motivation to perform the delinquent acts. All other things being equal, a youth is more likely to perform a delinquent act if motivated to do so rather than in the absence of such motivation. Further, a youth is more likely to perform a delinquent act if the anticipated satisfactions of important needs are greater, and the anticipated frustrations of important needs are fewer as a consequence of the delinquent behavior than would be the result of not performing the delinquent act. However, even if the person in balance expected satisfaction of important needs from the delinquent behavior, the youth might still not perform the delinquent act because of the absence of opportunity to do so.

The opportunity to perform the act includes physical, personal, and interpersonal resources as well as the situational context that provides the occasion and the stimulus for the delinquent behavior. The current situation provides a number of features that may stimulate overt acts, given a predisposition to commit some form of delinquent act. The opportunities presented by the person's current situation not only define the limits of what is possible but also stimulate latent dispositions, including dispositions to delinquent acts. A person who is disposed to violence may be stimulated to commit a violent act at a particular time when cues for violence (a gun, television programs) are present. A person who is disposed to steal may in fact steal when an appropriate object of value becomes apparent.

The youth's current situation and his motivation to perform delinquent acts influence each other. A person disposed to commit a delinquent act may seek out situational opportunities. On the other hand, the situation in which a youth finds himself may stimulate a preexisting disposition to commit a delinquent act. Hewitt has noted that under some condition, delinquent behavior occurs

in response to the demands of particular situations. Attacks upon one's person or self-esteem by other juveniles, challenges to masculine integrity that must be answered, the special hostility of police and other adults, threats by other delinquent groups, and similar events tend to precipitate episodes of delinquent behavior in which the risks are momentarily forgotten [1979: 97].

The discussion now turns to a consideration of the factors that influence the opportunities to perform delinquent behavior.

Generality of Deviant Dispositions

The range of opportunities that are available to the youth who is motivated to perform acts defined as deviant depends in part upon how general or specific the youth's motives are. A youth may be motivated to perform any of a range of illicit acts simply because they are illegal. The motive may stem from a history of experiences of failure and being rejected in the conventional world and from the consequent rejection of conventional morals. The motive is a general one in the sense that any of a range of delinquent behaviors would satisfy the need. Since any of several behaviors would satisfy the need, the opportunities to perform any of several patterns are greater than the opportunities to perform any one of them. If the person perceives the illicit use of drugs among peers in his environment and is able to procure the drugs, the youth will be more likely to perform this pattern. If patterns of interpersonal aggression are apparent and the youth has the physical prowess necessary to engage in such activities, then he is more likely to perform that act. However, the opportunities to perform one or the other of them are greater than the opportunities to perform one in particular.

Similarly, the youth's motivation to identify with and to be accepted by a group that endorses delinquent patterns can be satisfied by performing any of a range of delinquent behaviors. The opportunities to perform delinquent behaviors multiply as the range of behaviors that can satisfy the youth's needs increases. Or if acceptance by the group is dependent upon conforming to a generally stated standard such as being daring, then any of a number of illicit activities that have a high associated risk might serve the purpose of securing group approval. Once again, as the number of delinquent activities that might satisfy the youth's needs multiply, so do the potential opportunities for engaging in delinquent behavior. As the number of generally stated values increases, the opportunities to engage in delinquent activities increase even further.

> Simply being in the company of others—each with a degree of situational acceptance of delinquent behavior in the name of such socially valued ends as excitement, loyalty to friends, daring, retributive justice, or possession of expensive goods— is likely sometimes to result in misbehavior [Johnson, 1979: 59].

In contrast to the opportunities available to engage in any of the range of delinquent behaviors that might fulfill some more general need are the more limited opportunities to engage in one specific delinquent pattern that the youth anticipates will satisfy his needs. The opportunities to engage in illicit drug use are far fewer than the opportunities to engage in *either* drug use, vandalism, theft, or any other of a range of delinquent patterns.

Involvement in the Conventional Order

Involvement of the youth in conventional society is relevant to the availability of delinquent opportunities in three ways. First, it influences awareness of delinquent alternatives. Second, it influences the availability of motivationally more favorable response patterns. Third, involvement in conventional society provides adaptive response patterns that may predispose the person to particular forms of deviance.

Awareness of Delinquent Patterns

An essential feature of the opportunities to act out deviant dispositions is the youth's conceptual awareness of deviant patterns. It is not difficult to imagine that a youth might be socialized in a group that shares relatively homogeneous values. The child does not hear of deviant alternatives, let alone observe them. The behaviors, while not unknown to the guardians of conventional morals (otherwise they could not be defined as delinquent), may be unthinkable to the youths in the community in question. Even if the youth was disposed to deviate in some fashion from conventional values, certain specific delinquent patterns would not be available for the youth to act out since they were literally inconceivable.

However, even when the youth does learn to conceive of the delinquent pattern, on a day to day basis the continuing expenditure of time and effort in conventional activities precludes current awareness of delinquent activities. As Hirschi observes:

> The assumption. . . is that a person may be simply too busy doing conventional things to find time to engage in deviant behavior. The person involved in conventional activities is tied to appointments, deadlines, working hours, plans, and the like, so the opportunity to commit deviant behaviors rarely arises. To the extent that he is engrossed in conventional activities, he cannot even think about deviant acts, let alone act out his inclinations [1969: 22].

Conventional Opportunities

The disposition to behave according to delinquent values need not result in delinquent behavior even when the opportunities for delinquent behavior are possible. Because of the possible costs associated with delinquent behavior, the availability of normative response patterns that can serve the same functions as delinquent patterns may forestall delinquent behavior. If, for example, the failure to achieve the middle-class values to which one was committed leads to feelings of frustration, these feelings can be reduced by changing one's values to those of a less demanding set but one that is still acceptable within the context of the legal structure.

That more individuals from the lower stratum who are frustrated in the achievement of values endorsed by middle-class society do not become aware of and choose delinquent adaptations is possibly due to the alternative normative adaptations available to them. It is possible to retreat from the more inclusive conventional value system by endorsing a more limited value system, that of one's own class structure. Within the class structure, more attainable standards and the means to meet those standards permit an individual to achieve an acceptable level of self-evaluation. Hence, there is no need to become aware of and adopt modes of delinquent response that permit attainment of social values through illegal means, aggression against conventional values, or the adoption of delinquent standards of behavior as intrinsically valued substitutes for conventional standards.

The awareness and disposition of such alternative conventional responses (that preclude the need for delinquent responses) is a function of the degree to which the youth is involved in the conventional social structure.

Normal Adaptive Patterns

Which of a range of delinquent patterns will be adopted when the youth is disposed to perform delinquent behavior (whether out of a need to conform to expectations that endorse delinquent patterns or in response to the failure to conform to the standards of conventional society) will be affected also by the characteristic response patterns that the youth learns in the course of socialization in his membership groups. Where the youth is disposed to delinquent responses, he is more likely to adopt those specific delinquent responses that are compatible with his normal response dispositions. Indeed, frequently, the delinquent pattern appears to be an extreme response that in a less extreme degree would be acceptable in the context of the youth's membership groups. For example, certain delinquent responses, particularly those involving aggressive behavior, are more appropriate as extensions of the masculine rather than feminine role.

Awareness of Delinquent Patterns

The opportunities to act upon dispositions to deviant responses require awareness of delinquent patterns.

Longitudinal data collected from several thousand junior high school students in Houston (Kaplan, et al., 1984) support the idea that awareness of the opportunities available to perform deviant acts increases the likelihood of actually performing deviant acts. Youths in the eighth grade were more likely to report having performed delinquent acts (using or selling narcotic drugs, breaking and entering, vandalism, joy riding, personal assault, theft) if they had reported in the seventh grade an awareness of deviant opportunities (reports that many of the kids at school perform any of a number of specific deviant acts). It should be noted, however, that although this measure may reflect deviant opportunities, it may also reflect the perception of the activity being legitimate in their immediate peer environment.

Awareness of the delinquent patterns is influenced by the existence of stable delinquent response patterns in the environment and the interaction between the youth and those who perform the delinquent acts.

Delinquent Subcultures

The significance of the work of such observers as Cloward and Ohlin (1960) in the present context rests upon the suggestion that deviant opportunities structures exist in the social environment. In the urban slum areas, youths disposed to delinquency (because of their inability to achieve the conventional goals they aspired to through conventional means) were presented with different types of deviant opportunity structures in the form of deviant subcultures, which permit them to act out their deviant impulses. Cloward and Ohlin (1960) identified three important types of deviant subculture. The "criminal subculture" permitted the youth to learn how to be successful as a professional criminal. The "conflict subculture" provided aggressive response patterns directed toward conventional values that, in the absence of legitimate and illegitimate opportunities, the youths could not achieve. "Drug subcultures" permitted the youths to withdraw from the conventional value system in the face of the absence of viable opportunities to achieve these values or even to attack them (in the presence of internalized prohibitions against violence).

However, the description of the types of subcultures was not, perhaps, as important as the observation that ongoing delinquent response patterns exist as shared expectations among segments of the population. The interaction with those who share these expectations provides the opportunity for youths to act out their delinquent dispositions.

Delinquent Associates

The delinquent subculture would not provide the opportunity to act out delinquent motives if the youth did not associate, under favorable circumstances, with those who share the delinquent subculture. As noted earlier, being part of a delinquent group may be the result of being born into a subculture in which one necessarily interacts with individuals who share delinquent values. While the delinquent subculture may have its origin in being a collective response to shared frustrations on the part of members of a particular social stratum, these origins may be lost to the memories of current participants in the subculture. The individual participates in the delinquent subculture simply because the youth is really not aware of realistic alternatives. Everyday satisfaction depend upon conforming to the normative expectations (including the performance of delinquent acts) shared by members of the subculture.

Alternatively, and in addition to the foregoing, individuals may become attracted to delinquent subcultures as an individual adaptation to personal failure to achieve conventional values. Such an adaptation is made easier by the loss of emotional attachment to the conventional structure that results from the youth's perceived failure to achieve conventional values. This reasoning is consistent with observations by Johnson (1979) that school failure was directly associated with having friends who commit delinquent acts, and was associated with the loss of attachment to school values, which in turn was associated with having delinquent associates.

In addition, the forced interaction with delinquent youths may be the consequence of formal sanctions for initial delinquent acts. The sentencing of a delinquent youth to an institution increases interaction with other delinquents from whom he can learn the techniques of illicit activity both during and after institutionalization. The negative sanctions applied to the youth for committing a delinquent act, in effect, provide opportunity for such future acts that he might be disposed to perform.

Regardless of the means by which the youth comes to have delinquent associates, interaction with other delinquents does provide the opportunities to act in accordance with their deviant motivations. Delinquent associates serve as role models from whom the youth learns delinquent patterns. Where the delinquent activity requires company or someone to provide help, the delinquent associate fills the need.

One of the more consistent findings in the literature is a relationship between having friends who commit delinquent acts and commiting delinquent acts oneself (Hirschi, 1969; Hindelang, 1973; Conger, 1976; Johnson, 1979). Although these findings tend to be from cross-sectional studies, the role that delinquent associates play in the performance of delinquent behavior is suggested also by data reported from a longitudinal study of students during their junior high school years (Kaplan, et al., 1982). Among the findings was the report that students who felt rejected by their peers (the kids at school) were *less* likely to use drugs at a later point in time. In addition, students who felt rejected by the kids at school were less likely to perceive the other kids at school using drugs and were less likely to report that their good friends used drugs. These findings suggest that peer groups frequently provide the opportunities and the occasions for illicit use of drugs. When the person does not feel himself or herself to be part of the peer group, the occasions and the opportunities for illicit drug use are not available.

Responses to Delinquency

Both informal and formal responses to patterns of delinquency will influence subsequent opportunities to perform the act. The opportunities to commit crime are, in particular, influenced by the actions people take to ward off crime. If people out of fear avoid dark and dangerous places and stay home as much as possible, the opportunities for mugging incidents is diminished.

The opportunity for individuals who are motivated to perform delinquent responses also are dependent upon the public attitudes and upon the legislative and law enforcement activities that reflect those attitudes. If legislation provides strong sanctions against drug use, for example, and the legislation is strictly enforced, the pattern might become less prevalent. Less prevalent patterns are less likely to provide opportunities for being imitated. In addition, quite apart from any deterrent effect the legislative and enforcement patterns might have upon the behavior of the would-be drug user, these patterns might well have a deterrent effect upon the behavior of those who would supply the illicit substances. To the extent that the supply is limited, so is the opportunity for those who are motivated to do so to use the drugs.

SUMMARY

Whether or not a person actually performs the delinquent behavior that the youth is motivated to perform depends upon the strength of counteracting motives and the opportunities to perform the delinquent behavior. In the course of the socialization process, the youth learns to need the approval of other people, to conform to the role expectations associated with important social identities, to do what is right, and a variety of other experiences. If anticipated delinquent behavior and the consequences of that behavior appear to the youth to threaten the satisfaction of these needs, or if it appears that the needs will be better served by not performing the delinquent act, the youth will be somewhat restrained from acting delinquent. The extent to which these motives effectively restrain the youth from acting in accordance with his deviant motives depends upon the youth's attraction to the conventional social structure and the inability to justify the delinquent behavior in terms of conventional values.

Even in the absence of motives that counteract motivation to perform delinquent behavior, the youth will not perform the delinquent acts if opportunities to do so are not present. The availability of opportunities for delinquent behavior is a function, in part, of the number of different delinquent patterns that might fulfill the need. The opportunities to perform delinquent patterns increase as the number of such delinquent patterns increase.

The youth's opportunities to perform delinquent activities will be influenced by the extent of his or her involvement in conventional society. With increasing involvement in the conventional world, the person is less likely to become aware of delinquent patterns and is more likely to become aware of conventional patterns that present themselves as opportunities to satisfy the youth's needs. However, involvement in the conventional culture may at the same time influence the form that delinquent behavior would take in the absence of more favorable conventional response patterns. Many delinquent patterns are illegal extensions of conventional response patterns that are learned in the course of the socialization process.

The opportunities for delinquent behavior, while they are decreased by involvement with the conventional culture, are increased by the existence of stable delinquent response patterns and favorable interaction with those who share these response patterns. The delinquent associates provide the occasion and the means for engaging in the motivated delinquent behavior.

Finally, both informal and formal (law enforcement) responses to delinquent behavior affect the opportunities to perform the delinquent behavior. Effective law enforcement, for example, decreases the availability of role models from whom the delinquent patterns can be learned as well as of other means (for example, drug supply) that permit the performance of the delinquent act.

DISCUSSION QUESTIONS

1. Are particular kinds of delinquent responses associated with particular social categories? In less extreme forms are these responses proper ones for people in these social categories? Discuss with particular reference to gender-related and social class-related categories.

2. Which of the counteracting motives would be most effective in preventing violent behaviors, theft, vandalism?

3. What actions might be taken by parents, police, school authorities, or adolescent peers that would limit opportunities to engage in delinquent behaviors?

6

CONTINUITY OF
DELINQUENT BEHAVIOR

It is clear that there is a degree of stability between early delinquent behavior and later performance of illegal acts. The degree of association between early antisocial behavior and adult antisocial behavior appears to be greatest when the earlier measure is taken during middle adolescence (Gersten et al., 1976). It is also clear, however, that for a large (perhaps greater) portion of early delinquent performers, certain factors intervene to result in the discontinuity of deviant patterns between youth or adolescence and adulthood. For example, a follow-up study of elementary school children indicated that of those with histories of juvenile delinquency, 24.7 percent had adulthood offenses recorded compared to only 4.1 percent of those without a history of juvenile delinquency. Nevertheless, while there is a much greater probability of adult offenses among early delinquents, three out of four delinquents did not have a record of adult arrest (Roff, 1977).

What factors then account for the stability or increase, as opposed to the decrease, of antisocial behavior over time? Where stability in antisocial behavior is observed, is it accounted for by reinforcing social responses or the continuity of the same circumstances that led to the initial responses? Where instability in responses over time is noted, is this due to the absence of such reinforcing social responses or to the discontinuity of the circumstances that stimulated the initial delinquent responses? Certain of the factors that determine whether early delinquency will be continued or discontinued are related to the consequences of the early delinquent behavior, while other influences reflect changes in the youth's circumstances that are independent of the early delinquent behavior (ongoing developmental processes, for example).

Where the continuity or discontinuity of the delinquent behavior is the result of consequences of the early performance of the delinquent behavior, the relationship may be more or less direct. More directly, the youth may be motivated to continue or discontinue the behavior because of the immediate positive or negative consequences of the delinquent behavior itself. For example, the use of illicit drugs may cause the person to feel good about himself or to feel ill. The physical abuse of another person or the destruction of property may increase the person's sense of power. Engaging in gang fights may result in physical injury. These outcomes may positively reinforce or extinguish motivation to continue the behavior. Less directly, the factors that influence continuation or discontinuation of the deviant response (whether by reinforcing or extinguishing motives to behave in this way or by influencing opportunities for delinquent behaviors) are mediated by other consequences of the earlier delinquent behavior. Such consequences include the approving responses of delinquent associates, the disapproving responses of conventional groups, and the stigmatizing effects of formal sanctions.

The explanation of why youths continue or discontinue delinquent behavior is a complex one. Some of the youth's circumstances increase the likelihood while others decrease the likelihood that earlier delinquent behavior will be repeated or continued. The correct prediction of the outcome depends on an understanding of the balance of these circumstances. The discussion now considers in turn the circumstances that lead to continuation, or repetition, or increased involvement in delinquent behavior and those that lead to discontinuation or decreased involvement in delinquent behavior.

DETERMINANTS OF CONTINUATION
OF DELINQUENT BEHAVIOR

Once a youth has performed delinquent acts, what circumstances will lead to the continuation, repetition, or escalation of the youth's degree of involvement in delinquent activity? These circumstances may be distributed conveniently among three categories. The first set of circumstances includes those that provide positive reinforcement of the need to perform delinquent acts. The positive reinforcement stems from the satisfactions of important needs experienced by the youth as a result or the more or less direct consequences of the delinquent behavior. The second set includes those circumstances that weaken the effects of motives that previously deterred the youth from performing delinquent acts. The third set of circumstances increase or establish ongoing opportunities for the performance of delinquent behavior.

Positive Reinforcement of Delinquent Behavior

Delinquent behavior is self-reinforcing in two ways. First, the performance of delinquent behavior may satisfy important needs for the youth. Since the behavior satisfies the needs, as the needs continue or recur, the delinquent behavior will continue or be repeated in the expectations that the needs will still or once again be satisfied. Second, regardless of the motivation for the initial performance of the deviant behavior, the deviant behavior creates a need (specifically a need for self-justification) that is satisfied by continuation or repetition of the delinquent act or by the structuring of the social environment in ways that facilitate the continuation or repetition of the delinquent act. The difference between the two modes of self-reinforcement is that in the former instance, a need preceded the delinquent behavior that satisfied the need. In the latter case, the delinquent behavior *created* a need that is satisfied by repetition or continuation of the delinquent behavior.

Delinquent Acts and Needs Satisfaction

Frequently, the performance of deviant acts results in the satisfaction of the youth's needs. These satisfactions reinforce motives to perform the delinquent act. The various needs that the youth experiences have been subsumed under the more general need to feel positively about oneself (Kaplan, 1975, 1980, 1982). It has been argued that delinquent acts can help to satisfy this need in any of three ways. Delinquent behavior may permit the youth to avoid the source of his self-devaluing attitudes, or to substitute new sources of positive self-devaluing experiences, to attack the basis of his self-devaluing attitudes, or to substitute new sources of positive self-evaluation. Some research findings do suggest that under certain conditions (including those associated with gender and social class), earlier deviant behavior may be associated with later decreases in self-derogation. However, the researchers are quite cautious in interpreting these findings as firm evidence of a casual effect of deviant behavior upon improvement in self-attitudes (Kaplan, 1980; Kaplan et al., 1982, 1984).

The *avoidance* of self-devaluing experiences as a result of delinquent acts might occur through the enforced avoidance of the negative responses of people in the conventional environment. To the extent that the youth spends more time with delinquent peers, is incarcerated or is otherwise excluded from interacting with conventional others, he will necessarily avoid the negative reactions that he has experienced in the conventional environment in the past.

Delinquent acts that involve *attacks* upon conventional institutions or the representatives of these institutions may have self-enhancing consequences by causing the individual to express his rejection of the values by which he in the past rejected himself. Deprived of self-acceptance by being unable to approximate conventional standards and, consequently, to earn group approval, the youth would find rejection of the standards and of the group that rejected him to be gratifying. The delinquent behavior would signify that the standards by which he formerly rejected himself were invalid.

In addition to avoiding and attacking the sources of self-devaluing attitudes, delinquent activities may provide *new ways* in which the individual can evaluate himself positively. The delinquent activity may involve associating with a group that endorses standards which are more easily attainable than those endorsed in the conventional environment. The youth thus gains gratification from achieving the new standards. Further, sometimes rejection by others in conventional groups stimulates the need to be accepted by others. Toward the goal of being accepted by the group, the youth behaves in ways (including delinquent behaviors) that he perceives the group as endorsing. Presumably, conformity to delinquent group norms will result in acceptance by the group and will positively reinforce the value of the delinquent behavior that earned the acceptance. In fact, as Matza (1964) notes, it is not even necessary for delinquents to share beliefs in the rightness of their behavior for the beliefs to influence individual behavior. As long as each individual believes that the others think the behavior is correct and they are motivated to be accepted by the other members, they will continue to behave as if the group shared beliefs about the rightness of the behaviors.

In addition to the gratifications achieved from delinquent behavior that conforms to the standards of delinquent associates, the delinquent behavior may be positively reinforced as a result of any of a number of other consequences of the substitution of deviant sources of gratification for conventional ones. For example, delinquent activities may give the individual a new sense of power or control over his environment which leads him to think of himself as a more effective individual.

Delinquent Acts and Self-Justification

The initial performance of delinquent acts is threatening to the satisfaction of important needs of youths who were socialized in conventional society. Specifically, the youth feels a need to conform to moral standards and to be accepted by the community as one who conforms to those standards. Once the person has performed delinquent acts and thereby has threatened satisfaction of these needs, the person is motivated to behave in ways that reduce the distress associated with the threat to need-satisfaction. Among the ways the person can reduce the distress is, first, by justifying the act in conventional terms, and, second, by transforming the youth's identities in ways that justify the behavior as appropriate to the new (deviant) identity. Both sets of self-justifying responses involve the continuation, repetition, or escalation of deviant involvement.

Justification in conventional terms. The initial performance of delinquent behavior appears to require justification by youths who were raised in conventional society. Data consistent with this assertion are reported by Tittle (1980) from a survey of 1993 individuals from New Jersey, Iowa, and Oregon. People who report having performed delinquent acts are less likely to judge the acts as serious, as morally wrong, and (particularly for some kinds of acts) as justifying the enactment of laws against the acts. For example, 20 percent of those who reported smoking marijuana in the past judged the act to be morally wrong, compared with 73 percent of those who had not committed the act in the past; 20 percent of those who reported smoking marijuana in the past described the offense as a serious one for people like them, compared to 78 percent of those who reported that they had not committed the offense in the past; and, only 25 percent of those who reported smoking marijuana in the past thought it ought to be against the law, compared with 75 percent of those who had not committed the act in the past.

Of course, these data might also indicate that beliefs in the moral legitimacy of the act have faciliated past performance of the act. Nevertheless, these data are consistent with the position that past performance of the act motivates the individual to justify the act to himself. It seems reasonable to expect that such justification would then faciliate the continued performance of the act.

The justification of the delinquent behavior in conventional terms is faciliated by the availability of collective justifications by delinquent associates and by the prevalance of the behavior in the society. The collective justifications serve both the youth who was reared in a delinquent subculture and the youth who was raised in more conventional groups. Where the youth was raised in a subculture that endorses delinquent acts, of course, collective self-justifications are plentiful. If the worthiness of the delinquent act was challenged by representatives of the conventional culture, the force of subcultural tradition would justify the act. Such behavior patterns reflect intrinsically valued group standards conformity to which evokes positive sanctions and deviation from which evokes negative sanctions from group members. In like manner, if a person who was raised in the more conventional society comes to commit an act that he himself in the past defined as delinquent, the repetition or continuity of the pattern requires that the youth justify the activity (they deserved what I did to them), a personal justification that is made easier when the youth may associate himself with others who have collectively devised good reasons for the performance of the delinquent patterns.

The prevalance of an illicit pattern provides the self-justification that, "everybody does it." So widespread are illicit acts of violence (to say nothing of the prevalance of legitimate violence) that such acts are within the realm of expected events and are greeted by the general public with passive resignation. Against this background, it is not surprising that a youth who becomes motivated to and has performed an illicit act of violence feels less constrained by motives of morality from repeating the act in the future.

The justification of the act in conventional terms required by the youth's socialization experiences facilitates repetition or continuation of earlier delinquent acts. The repetition of the delinquent behavior, in turn, testifies to the youth's belief in the legitimacy of the act.

Acceptance of deviant identities. The consequences of earlier delinquent acts frequently lead the person to question his self-worth. In order to restore his feelings of self-acceptance, the person adopts a deviant identity and conforms to behaviors that he sees as validating that identity. This process has been most often described from what others have termed the labeling perspective.

Consistent with the idea that being labeled as an offender (as reflected in self-report of having been arrested) increases the likelihood of future performance of the act, Tittle (1980) reported data indicating that having been arrested is related to self-reports of some future probability of performing specified deviant acts, including theft of $50, marijuana smoking, and assault. From this perspective, the earlier and later deviant acts are mediated by the fact that a major basis for the interaction of others with the youth on both formal and informal levels is the recognition by others that the youth has committed a delinquent act. On the formal level, the investigation and adjudication process is influenced.

> Persons with criminal histories are more likely to be suspected of crime. If arrested, they are more likely to be found guilty. This occurs both through the impediment that prior record poses for access to bail and adequate legal representation and through its direct influence on the court's assessment of guilt. Finally, the additional conviction becomes part of the defendant's records; in future contacts with the law, it too will contribute to the growing presumption of guilt with which they are processed [Farrell and Swigert, 1982: 79].

On an informal level the ensuing rejection of the youth who is stigmatized may take the form of denying the person access to informal associations with family members and conventional friends, denial of employment opportunities, and increased suspicion of even nondeviant activities performed by the youth who has been stigmatized. The youth is unable to engage in intrinsically valued activities and in those activities that constitute means to the achievement of other valued ends. Consequently, the youth is deprived of the ability to behave in ways that would evoke rewards from the conventional society. He must necessarily continue to seek achievable values and the means by which those values may be achieved from nonconventional relationships.

If a youth's interactions with others are based predominantly on the others' knowledge of the youth's earlier delinquency, the youth will be increasingly likely to think of himself in these same terms. As more and more people interact with the youth on this basis, he will conceive of himself in terms of the performance of delinquent activities. Further, if others consistently interact with him in terms of these activities, the youth will be unable to ignore this feature of himself. The delinquent activities will be a more salient, central, *undeniable* part of the youth's self-image.

Since it is such an important part of himself, how he evaluates the delinquent behavior will affect greatly how he evaluates himself in general. Since everyone needs to feel positively about himself, the youth will try to structure his environment in ways that make the delinquent activities a more valued than disvalued aspect of himself. If some of the people with whom he interacts respond to the delinquent activity positively while others respond negatively, the youth, in all likelihood, and insofar as he has control of these processes, will structure his patterns of interaction so as to minimize interaction with those who respond negatively and to maximize interaction with those who respond positively. He will do this because those who respond positively or in support of his delinquent activities make it easier for him to feel good about himself (a pleasurable activity), and he comes to take pleasure in interacting with them; and because those who respond negatively to his delinquent activities (a central feature of the youth's self-image) make it more difficult for him to like himself as he needs to do and, consequently, interacting with them will be experienced as distressful. The result of this process will be a positive experience associated with a delinquent self-image and continued performance of delinquent behavior that is required by the now satisfying self-image.

If most other people did not act toward the youth in terms of his delinquent activity (because the delinquent activity was considered by others as the most prominent part of his activity), then the youth would be able to deny this aspect of himself when it had undesirable consequences. He would feel free to perceive himself in terms of more conventional features of himself and would not feel the need to avoid interacting with representatives of the conventional order. Positive self-feelings could be pursued through the acceptance and achievement of conventional values rather than through self-justification of a delinquent self-image by continued, repeated, or escalated involvement in delinquent behavior.

Weakening of Social Controls

The motives that restrain a youth from initially performing delinquent acts (the need for the positive consequences of not performing delinquent acts and fear of the negative consequences that might occur if the delinquent act were performed) frequently are weakened by the consequences of early performance of the act. As a result, the loss of fear of adverse consequences and the weakening of the attraction to the rewards of conformity permit continued involvement in the delinquent activity.

Limited Adverse Consequences

As a result of earlier performance of delinquent acts, whether the act is or is not detected, the youth may well have experiences that decrease the expectation of adverse consequences. Where the act is detected, the youth may well observe that few of the anticipated adverse consequences in fact occurred.

As Tittle observes:

> Interestingly enough, it is usually the case that nothing much
> at all happens when rules are broken. Moral crises are usually
> avoided by rationalization, and the triviality of most deviance
> is revealed when rule violation produces no great catastrophes.
> Indeed,. . . there is rarely even apprehension and punishment
> of the rule breaker. Hence, those who for one reason or
> another actually do break the rules usually discover that most
> of their fears were ungrounded. Once an act has been commit-
> ted and successfully rationalized it no longer appears as moral-
> ly reprehensible as before and once an act is seen by experience
> to be less serious than thought one accords it much less impor-
> tance in the future. . . . Moreover, once the shell of illusion
> has been broken for some rules one is likely to have less
> reverence for other rules. [1980: 67-69].

When the initial delinquency is observed and harshly respond-
ed to, the youth is effectively expelled from conventional
society and, hence, the interaction between the youth and
representatives of conventional society is markedly reduced.
The youth may be detained in an institution or simply be
denied the privileges of informal interaction with family
members, neighbors, or former friends. Paradoxically, these
acts of expulsion that serve as negative sanctions for the
earlier delinquency effectively preclude the observation of
further wrongdoing and, therefore, the administration of further punishments for the delinquent acts. By expelling the
youth from society, he is removed from the surveillance of
those who might prevent him from future wrongdoing by
punishing the delinquent acts as they are observed.

Decreased Attraction to Conventional Values

The attraction to the values of conventional society and
to membership in conventional groups as a basis for positive
self-evaluation is weakened both by the very same processes

that influenced the youth's initial motivation to perform deviant acts and by the responses of society to the initial deviance.

The inability of the youth to succeed by conventional standards leads to negative self-attitudes and to the disposition to perform deviant acts that might lead to more positive self-feelings. At the same time, the youth's association, in his own mind, between the distressful self-rejecting attitudes and the conventional standards that are the measure of the youth's failure decreases the youth's attraction to these standards. Hence, any impulses to delinquency that the youth experiences are less likely to be restrained as they were formerly by the attraction to the conventional standards.

In addition, the early performance of the delinquent acts has consequences that more or less directly lead the youth to reject conventional standards that ordinarily would help to restrain delinquent impulses. A number of research findings confirms the adverse consequences of early delinquent behavior. For example, Elliott and Voss, in a longitudinal study of the ninth graders who were followed annually until the usual date of high school graduation, "recognize that delinquent activity is itself a *cause* of conflict and alienation in the home and school and leads delinquent youth to seek other delinquent juveniles as associates" (Elliott and Voss, 1974: 203, italics in original). Compatible findings were reported by Kaplan and his associates (1982) using data from a longitudinal study of junior high school students. Among other findings, it was observed that youths whose friends got into trouble later felt that they were rejected by family and rejected in the school environment.

The informal rejection by family or school, and the stigma associated with being the object of more formal sanctions such as being arrested reflect intrinsically distressful experiences and barriers to the achievement of other emotionally significant goals. On the one hand, the shame of being punished for certain infractions leads to a self-defensive rejection of the moral standards. The youth, who recognizes that the delinquent behavior is an inescapable part of his public image and, over time, becomes an accepted part of his self-image, is motivated by the need to evaluate himself positively to create personal justifications for the behavior and to ally himself with those who can offer collective justifications for the behavior. On the other hand, the rejection of the youth by members of conventional society deprives the youth of access to resources that, besides being intrinsically valued, are means to the achievement of other valued ends. Such resources include a good job and the trust and respect of others. As a result, the youth is decreasingly attracted to the normative order. Simply put, the youth no longer cares, or does not care as much, what the representatives of the conventional order think about his behavior. Since he does not care, the attitudes of others no longer constrain him from performing a delinquent act that he otherwise is motivated to perform. Rather, the youth becomes increasingly dependent upon delinquent associates for standards of self-evaluation and for the resources for achieving the standards.

Opportunities for Delinquency

The early performance of delinquent acts frequently has consequences that increase the youth's opportunity to perform delinquent acts. As a result of the youth's rejection of and by the conventional society (considered above), the youth becomes increasingly attracted to delinquent associates and increases the amount of social interaction with other delinquents. Some of this interaction with delinquent associates is the necessary result of periods of detention in custodial halls. The increased interaction increases the opportunities to observe and learn delinquent patterns in addition to being provided with numerous occasions when the enactment of the deviant behavior would be called for. With increasing interaction comes the motivation to conform to the expectations of delinquent associates upon whom the youth depends for satisfaction of his day-to-day needs. As the youth becomes symbolically and physically separated from conventional society, he or she depends upon delinquent associates for an increasingly greater proportion of the opportunities to satisfy the youth's needs. Perhaps consistent with this conclusion, Johnson (1979) reports that among youths who had come to the attention of the authorities, failure in school was associated with self-reports of delinquent acts to a greater extent than among youths who had not previously come to the attention of the authorities. Although other interpretations are possible, this may indicate that those who have been labelled as law violators may find that they have no alternative ways of dealing with failure other than continued violations of the law. On the other hand, those who have not been labelled as law violators may still have the option of using more conventional ways of dealing with school failure.

DETERMINANTS OF DISCONTINUATION
OF DELINQUENT BEHAVIOR

Just as different factors influence the continuation, repetition, or escalation of delinquent activity, so may any of a variety of circumstances influence the discontinuation or decreased involvement in delinquent activity. As when discussing the continuation of delinquent activity, three different sets of circumstances will be considered: failure of delinquent activities to satisfy the youth's needs (the absence of positive reinforcement); adverse consequences of delinquent acts which threaten continuing satisfaction of the youth's needs; and changes in the youth's needs or opportunities to meet those needs that render delinquent behaviors unnecessary.

Absence of Positive Reinforcement

Delinquent behaviors frequently are more or less successful attempts to meet the needs of the youth. Some of these needs arise out of failure of a youth to successfully achieve what he is expected to by self and others. The delinquent behavior reflects attempts to avoid or attack the conventional standards according to which the youth must be judged a failure, or to provide substitute standards that might more easily be achieved in order to earn self-approval and approval by others. As noted above, where the delinquent patterns successfully serve these functions and satisfy the youth's needs, the motivation to continue the delinquent behavior will be reinforced.

However, it has been argued that frequently the delinquent behavior fails to satisfy the youth's needs and, thereby, to positively reinforce the delinquent behavior. John P. Hewitt commenting on delinquent gangs in this connection observes that the gang member is quite unlikely to experience satisfaction of his needs in these settings.

> The delinquent peer group provides only unsatisfactory solutions to its members' problems. Self-esteem is seldom found in this context because there are few or no norms governing conduct for which favorable evaluations can be received and translated into self-esteem. How can self-esteem be based upon behavior that, even though it may win applause from peers, can not be defended in terms of rightness but only rationalized? How much self-esteem can be garnered in the company of peers whose own quest for self-esteem lead them to engage incessantly in the derogation of others? Although the motive underlying the juvenile's attachment to peers may be his quest for self-esteem, it is apparent that the peer group is the least likely place in which to find what he wants [1980: 98].

In any case, whether the inability of the youth to conform to delinquent group norms (if in fact such norms exist) is rare or common, when this situation does arise, the youth will fail to experience a sense of satisfaction, and on the contrary will experience a sense of failure and will be the object of negative sanctions from other group members. As a result, by the same processes that lead to any deviant disposition, the youth loses motivation to conform to and acquires motivation to deviate from the delinquent group norms. When alternative conventional standards that offer promises of achievement are presented, the youth who is motivated to drop delinquent patterns will do so.

Just as youths may adopt delinquent values and perform delinquent acts because of a failure in achieving conventional values, so may youth's who were socialized to accept delinquent behavior as proper be disposed to *reject* delinquent values if they are not able to be successful according to these standards. Just as we might predict that individuals who were not successful in achieving conventional values would be more likely to commit delinquent acts than youths who were successful in achieving conventional values, so would we predict that youths reared in subcultures that endorse delinquent acts would be less likely to be motivated to continue performance of the delinquent acts if they were unsuccessful in achieving the values. If the youth gained rewards to the extent that he was tough, able to con others, willing to take risks, and independent (Miller, 1958), but because of absence of personal abilities and internal constraints was unable to display these qualities and was, therefore, rejected, he would be likely to be motivated to reject the delinquent standards according to which he failed. Given this motivation, if he were presented with the opportunity to succeed according to another set of values, he would be a good candidate for disengaging from the delinquency-endorsing subculture. However, as in the instance of a person who becomes disposed to reject conventional values, continuation of the newly adopted behavior would be at risk since the earlier set of values continues to exert some influence upon the youth and mitigates the tendency to continue violating the earlier set of values.

Adverse Consequences

Not only might a youth discontinue delinquent behavior because the youth was unable to satisfy the needs (for self-esteem, to be accepted by other group members) that he anticipated would be satisfied through performing such behavior, but he might also be moved to cease delinquent behaviors because of consequences that threatened the satisfaction of other needs. Among the needs that are awakened by the consequences of initial performance of the delinquent acts are the discomfort experienced by the violation of conventional values to which the youth continues to remain committed, and the fear of formal sanctions.

Emotional Commitment to Conventional Values

A major source of motivations that counteract or mitigate the disposition to delinquency is the early adoption of conventional values in the course of the socialization process. It was noted earlier that individuals who have failed to achieve the values they learned in the course of the socialization process may adapt in any of a number of ways including using delinquent behaviors to achieve conventional values, withdrawing from the conventional world, and rejecting the validity of the values. However, these adaptations are potentially unstable because the youths have great difficulty in totally ridding themselves of the standards of behavior that they were taught to use in evaluating themselves. As Kobrin (1951) observes, the emotions accompanying hostile responses of young males in high delinquency areas to representatives of the conventional culture signify that the conventional values that they failed to achieve are important to them as criteria for evaluating themselves. It is just because of how badly they feel when they fail to achieve the values that they reject the values. The youth's gestures of defiance and contempt for the conventional order that frequently accompanies delinquent acts

is a dramatically exaggerated denial of a system of values *which the delinquent has at least partially introjected,* but which for the sake of preserving a tolerable self-image, he must reject. In this interplay of attitudinal elements, the vigor of the rejection of the value system is *the measure of its hold upon the person* [Kobrin, 1951: 660; italics not in the original].

It is precisely the strength of these values that makes the delinquent responses unstable. As long as the youth, while apparently rejecting the values, continues to feel strongly about the values, he will feel some discomfort while performing delinquent acts; and, given the opportunity to successfully pursue conventional values, the youth is likely to cease being attracted to and performing delinquent acts.

This situation is in contrast to that of the professional thief who uses different criteria for self-evaluation than those of the conventional society and, therefore, is less vulnerable to the negative judgment of representatives of conventional society. Because he does not reject himself for performing the delinquent act, he is less likely to discontinue the behavior than the youths who have ambivalent attitudes toward their delinquent behavior.

Fear of Formal Sanctions

The repetition of illegal acts is more likely to be prevented by the threat of arrest than is the initial performance of the deviant acts. Tittle (1980) reports data that in fact suggest that relative deterrence is greater for people who had already committed the criminal act in recent years. This finding, in conjunction with the finding that relative deterrence was greater for highly motivated individuals who are contemplating serious offenses, leads Tittle to conclude that, "formal sanction threats may actually be most effective for precisely those segments of the population for whom they are primarily designed" (1980: 264).

Other data suggest that the deterrent effect of formal sanctions may be stronger after initial experience of the sanctions. Certain of the data reported by Tittle do suggest that being arrested increases the effect of fear of sanctions for committing delinquent acts whether because the prior punishment magnifies the fear of the sanction or increases the recognition that sanctions might occur.

Changes in Needs and Opportunities

Since delinquent behavior frequently reflects attempts to satisfy needs, it is to be expected that changes in the person's needs or the opportunities to meet those needs will make delinquent behavior unnecessary. The changes may be precipitated by consequences of the delinquent behavior, purposive intervention, or normal maturational processes.

Consequences of Delinquent Behavior

Often the youth will experience an increase in perceived personal resources as a result of delinquent behavior that might render such behavior obsolete. For example, a possible consequence of delinquency that may lead to discontinuance of delinquent acts is the feeling of performing a daring act. The successful completion of such acts might lead the individual to have faith in his own ability to achieve more conventional goals through the use of conventional means.

Alternatively, a delinquent act may lead to a change in needs and, therefore, to a reduction in the delinquent behaviors that constituted attempts to cope with the failure to satisfy those needs. In this connection, data reported by Elliott (1966) and later by Elliott and Voss (1974) suggest that in lower socioeconomic status areas, students who drop out of school have much lower delinquency referral rates while out of school than they did while they were still in school and, indeed, had lower delinquency referral rates after dropping out than students who graduated. The results are what would be expected if the source of the youth's motivation to perform delinquent acts was the inability to achieve according to the middle class standards that characterize the public school system. When the youths dropped out, however, they presumably became less committed to self-evaluation according to middle-class standards and were able to evaluate themselves more favorably according to their own group standards, thus reducing the need for delinquent adaptations that would permit them to avoid, attack, or substitute delinquent standards for conventional values.

Purposive Intervention

Studies have reported that where offenders are provided with conventional opportunities to achieve conventional goals, the probability of repeated delinquent activity is reduced. Odell (1974) found from a study of juvenile offenders that different strategies of supervised probation had markedly different results regarding the likelihood of repeating delinquent offenses. Youths who had access to opportunities for educational and occupational advancement were appreciably less likely over a nine month period to repeat delinquent offenses than youths who participated in traditional casework and counseling programs. Equivalent results were observed for adult offenders who were part of an experimental program involving the assignment of former prisoners to income assistance and job placement programs (Berk et al., 1980). During the year following release, those former prisoners who received employment assistance or income supplements had fewer problems with the law than those who did not receive the employment income assistance.

Normal Maturation

By the very process of growing up, the youth gains opportunities to approximate the goals that he has been taught to value. As Hewitt notes, the fact that about two-thirds of all delinquents reform voluntarily by the age of twenty suggests that reform is associated with rewards that come with maturity. As the boy reaches maturity, he is able to work and engage in long-term heterosexual relationships.

In other words, jobs and girls provide what peers cannot: money, satisfaction and recognition based on work, and interpersonal relationships in which intimacy and rewarding interaction replace challenge and anxiety. As juveniles discover new capabilities they find them more rewarding than gang activities, and they alter their behavioral orientations, cease delinquent behavior, and begin to recover commitment to conventional norms of the lower-stratum society [1970: 98-99].

Tittle (1980) reports data that strongly support the notion that individuals who reach the age when they can achieve in a greater number of spheres have less need to commit delinquent acts. This is the case whether considering actual performance of delinquency or projected future performance of delinquent acts, and whether or not the individual had delinquent associates when he was growing up. Thus, among the people who reported not having delinquent associates, 11 percent of those aged 15 to 24, compared with only 4 percent of those aged 25 to 44, reported having committed a $50 theft within the past five years, and 15 percent of those aged 15 to 24, compared with only 5 percent of those aged 25 to 44, reported having committed assault within the last five years. The comparable figures for those who reported having delinquent associates were 18 percent and 9 percent for having committed a $50 theft within the last five years, and 32 percent and 15 percent for having committed assault within the last five years. The figures for projected future violations were quite comparable.

SUMMARY

Among youths who perform delinquent acts, the great majority will decrease their involvement in delinquent activities, although an appreciable number of youths will continue to perform delinquent behavior. Youths are simultaneously exposed to a number of influences, some of which increase and others of which decrease the probability that delinquent activities will continue, be repeated, or escalate. The balance of these influences will determine whether the youth in fact continues, repeats, or increases delinquent activity, on the one hand, or decreases or discontinues delinquent behaviors on the other hand.

Delinquent behavior is likely to continue if the youths associate increased need satisfaction with the delinquent behavior, if the youths experience a weakening of the motives that ordinarily act to constrain delinquent behavior, and if the opportunities for delinquent behavior remain apparent or increase. Delinquent behavior may satisfy the youth's needs in any of a number of ways: by permitting the youth to attack, avoid, or substitute delinquent standards for conventional standards that are the measure of the youth's failure; by allowing the youth to conform to the expectations of a positive reference group (delinquent associates); or by validating the acceptability of earlier delinquent behavior or of the deviant identity that is a consequence of the earlier delinquent behavior. The weakening of the social controls is attributed to the absence of visible adverse consequences of earlier delinquent behavior and of the decreased attraction to conventional values resulting from (1) the ongoing processes that influenced delinquent dispositions in the past and (2) the rejecting responses of conventional groups to the youth following initial delinquency. The youth's rejection of and by the conventional society increases the youth's attraction to and interaction with delinquent associates—processes that provide the occasions and opportunities for delinquent responses.

Delinquent behavior is likely to decrease or to be discontinued if the delinquent patterns do not appear to satisfy the needs that stimulated the delinquent responses, if the delinquent behaviors stimulate threats to the satisfaction of other needs (such as those associated with continuing emotional commitment to conventional morality or fear of formal sanctions), and if changes in the youth's needs or in the available conventional opportunities to satisfy those needs render delinquent behaviors superfluous.

DISCUSSION QUESTIONS

1. Discuss the relative advantages of and disadvantages of harsh penalties for initial delinquent behavior if the goal

is to decrease the number of first time offenders and if the goal is to decrease the number of hardened criminals.

2. Why do so many people who committed delinquent acts in their youth fail to commit criminal acts as adults?

3. What consequences of serving time for delinquent behaviors increase the likelihood of repeat offenses and what consequences decrease the probability of repeat offenses?

7

CONSEQUENCES OF DELINQUENCY

Although the primary focus of this volume is upon the onset and continuity of delinquent behavior, some consideration needs to be given to the social consequences of juvenile delinquency as well. This is the case not only because of the intrinsic interest of social scientists in this topic but also because the social consequences of delinquent behavior are themselves indirect influences upon the development and continuity of delinquent patterns.

Three sets of consequences of juvenile delinquency will be considered: formal and informal social responses to delinquent behavior; social functioning and reaffirmation of moral standards; and social change in the definition and prevalence of juvenile delinquency. These three sets of consequences influence each other and the future performance of delinquent behavior.

FORMAL AND INFORMAL SOCIAL RESPONSES

Social Responses to Delinquent Behavior

Among the significant social consequences of delinquent behavior are the formal and informal responses of community agencies and groups. The occurrence of acts of juvenile delinquency, when they come to the attention of representatives of the formal institutions of our society, stimulate a programmed series of activities involving investigation of the crime, arrest of alleged perpetrators, judicial decisions about guilt or innocence of the accused, and, if guilty, the administration of negative sanctions. Mediating the relationship between patterns of crime and such formal responses are the attitudinal responses of the public (particularly the emotion of fear), the less formal collective responses to the stimulation of fear (including petitions to legislatures, organization of neighborhood watch groups, taking other precautions, and, in rare instances, vigilante action), and the awareness of the crimes that stimulate the fear response.

The fear response might be evoked by either direct (personal experience with crime) or secondhand experiences (via mass media and interpersonal communication networks) with crime. Regarding the less direct experience, Skogan and Maxfield (1981: 260) observe:

> Our analyses found that the crucial linkage between those conversations about crime and fear was the information such talk brought them about local events. When people knew of crime in their areas, they were more afraid. Further, gossip about crime seems to magnify some of its more fear-provoking features. Stories about personal crimes seem to spread further than those concerning property crime, magnifying the relative frequency of violence. Stories about women and elderly victims seem to travel further than those describing more typical victims of personal crimes. Finally, when people hear about victims like themselves, they are even more fearful as a consequence.

Although serious crimes may be relatively rare, conversations about crime abound and occur in low crime areas as well as in high crime areas. This probably accounts in part for the fact that people who live in low crime areas also are afraid of crime. The judgment that personal crime was a big problem in the neighborhood represented the strongest predictor of fear. Skogan and Maxfield (1981) cite Furstenberg's (1971: 607) observation that "people take their cues from the neighborhood about how afraid to be."

Moderating Factors

The nature of the social responses, to the delinquent acts depend upon characteristics of the offense, the offender, and the victim.

Offenses

The responses of others to an offense are conditioned by characteristics of the crime. Crimes involving serious physical injury or rape are the most traumatic in their effect. Those crimes that were rated by the public as most serious were those that were least frequently performed. However, while less serious crimes have less impact on fear, because of the greater frequency of the crime, the *aggregate* effect of the crime (burglary is a case in point) might be quite large since it spreads concern about being victimized by a crime to places that otherwise might not experience serious crime. Burglary is widely distributed in the population, in wealthy and low-income areas, among whites as well as among blacks (Skogan and Maxfield, 1981).

Offenders

The nature of social responses to crime also vary according to the social characteristics of the offender. Among those who commit the same kind of delinquent act, people of one race, for example, may be more likely to be arrested, tried, and to receive more severe punishments than people of another race. Frequently, it is difficult to determine whether such an observation reflects the true nature of the rule (that is, people of one race are more strictly forbidden from performing the act than people of another race), the relative powerlessness of particular groups (people of one race have fewer resources which may be used effectively to forestall or mitigate the administration of legal sanctions than people of another race), or both factors.

Victims

Both the experience of the fear reaction to delinquency and the consequent collective reactions are influenced by the characteristics of the most likely victims of crime. Thus, physical and social vulnerability to crime is associated with fear of crime. Physical vulnerability involves the inability to resist attack (reflected, for example, in being older and female) and is more strongly related to fear than measures of social vulnerability which indicates frequent exposure to the threat of victimization (for example, being black and poor).

Patterns of response to crime that involve the protecting of one's household through measures designed to make it harder to break into the household undetected are not, surprisingly enough, directly related to the risk of being the victim of crime. Paradoxically, it has been found that those who lived in neighborhoods in which there were closer social ties and which were characterized by more economic resources were more likely to undertake such household protection measures as putting bars on windows and arranging for surveillance of the neighborhood (Skogan and Maxfield, 1981). Thus, those who were least vulnerable to becoming victims of crime were most likely to undertake protective responses to crime.

Consequences for Delinquency

The future performance of delinquent acts may be influenced by the formal and informal responses to earlier acts of juvenile delinquency. Part of this influence is mediated by the effects of the responses with regard to the reaffirmation of the moral code of the community. This will be considered in the following section. More directly, however, these responses, including the administration of more or less severe punishment and precautionary measures, may deter the youth from acting out a disposition or limit the opportunites to do so. Perhaps a person otherwise motivated to perform a delinquent act would not if he anticipated swift and sure punishment. He would also be less likely to act out a disposition to steal if the goods were not easily available. The influence of counteracting motives and limited opportunities on the acting out of deviant dispositions and on the continuity of deviant dispositions was discussed in Chapters 5 and 6. In the present context, however, it is perhaps appropriate to emphasize that the very actions that are intended to prevent repetition of being a victim (and may well do so for the people that engage in the tactic) may have little effect on the level of crime in the community as a whole.

> These precautionary tactics... leave potential offenders untroubled, displacing their attention onto others who are less watchful. Further, the atomizing effects of crime may further undermine the ability of a community to exercise any semblance of order. Where people are suspicious, avoid social contact, and surrender their interest in public facilities, it is impossible to rely upon informal social control mechanisms to control youths and suspicious persons [Skogan and Maxfield, 1981: 262-263].

In short, the measures taken by individuals for their own protection may actually function to decrease neighborhood surveillance and, thereby decrease the deterrent effect of fear of apprehension and increase the opportunities to perform delinquent acts.

SOCIAL FUNCTIONING AND REAFFIRMATION OF MORAL STANDARDS

The performance of delinquent acts and collective responses to those acts influence the functioning of the social system. Certain of these influences appear to be disruptive of social functioning while other consequences are thought to contribute to social cohesiveness.

Disruptive Consequences

Delinquent patterns and the social responses evoked by them adversely affect the social functioning of the delinquent, social functioning of those with whom the delinquent would ordinarily interact, the social functioning of the victims of the delinquency, and the communitywide achievement of social values.

The social functioning of the delinquent is disrupted in the sense that among the immediate negative consequences of deviant behavior is the displacement of normative activities by deviant activities. Not only is the performance of current roles lost, but the normal socialization process is interrupted so that the delinquent behavior forestalls the learning and performance of adult roles as well (Hewitt, 1970).

The social functioning of others who would ordinarily act as role partners with the delinquent is similarly disrupted. The proper performance of one's roles depends upon the proper performance of social roles on the part of those with whom the person interacts in the context of social relationships.

The appropriate performance of social roles on the part of victims is disrupted by the self-protective devices they use to decrease the risk of being a victim. Responses by the potential victims included such personal precautions as walking with others, driving as opposed to walking after dark, avoiding dangerous places, or staying home. Such responses in turn place constraints upon the amount of social interaction people may enjoy. "They may be forced to forgo opportunities for employment, recreation, and even simple social contact. Staying at home—being a true 'prisoner of fear'—may be the most significant consequence" (Skogan and Maxfield, 1981: 262).

To be sure, these costs must be weighed against the benefit of avoiding becoming a victim of crime. Although staying at home may decrease use of community facilities, at the same time, it reduces vulnerability to burglary. Nevertheless, the constraints on social functioning are costs that would not exist in the absence of juvenile delinquency.

The achievement of social values is hindered both by displacement of resources and the threats to these values posed by the social reactions to juvenile delinquency in the service of other values. Extensive juvenile delinquency requires the expenditures of scarce resources in order to protect those who conform to conventional norms. These costs are expended on such things as prisons and the personnel to man them, and on the judicial system and the cost of operating it. If the resources must be used in these ways, they cannot be used to achieve other social values.

Responses to juvenile delinquency also adversely influence the achievement of social values by occasioning circumstances that reflect violation of certain consensual expectations. The effect of citizen involvement in anti-crime activity upon racial or ethnic tolerance is a case in point. The following observations in this regard are based on findings from studies carried out in three cities (Chicago, Philadelphia, and San Francisco). Data were gathered by interviews with thousands of people, Census Bureau data, field observers stationed in selected neighborhoods, and analyses of newspaper content.

> In our most integrated neighborhood, South Philadelphia, bands of white toughs actively control the boundaries of Black enclaves. While this may serve to keep "strangers" out of the community, and to reduce conflict over appropriate standards of behavior there, this model of crime prevention surely has racist implications. In none of our cities is it entirely clear where social control to prevent crime and social control to stabilize the current distribution of ethnic and racial turf begin and end [Skogan and Maxfield, 1981: 265].

The ultimate cost of delinquency for social functioning is difficult to assess. It is possible, for example, that the

fear generated by delinquency may influence residential distribution patterns. Since the amount of crime in a community
is rated as an important consideration in the decision where
to move, once the decision to move has been made, crime
may be a factor in the exodus from the central city since
crime rates are in fact much lower outside the central city.
Surburban development, in turn, has profound consequences
for the central city.

> The metropolitan area has been segregated on the basis of
> class and race, concentrating in the city those who can least
> afford to support the social overhead this entails. The tax
> base, new investment, and desirable new jobs have fled. While
> not necessarily *caused* by crime, all of this has implications
> for inner-city conditions, most of them negative [Skogan and
> Maxfield, 1981: 266].

AFFIRMATION OF MORAL STANDARDS

In 1904, Emile Durkheim introduced in *The Rules of
Sociological Method* the idea that behavior defined as deviant
stands in contrast to collective normative expectations and
so functions to define collective normative standards. Farrell
and Swigert expand upon this idea as follows:

> Property is valued, for example, not only because respect
> for it is engendered by institutional efforts at socialization
> but also because the propertyless are shamed and the thief
> imprisoned. In much the same way as the moral leader ex-
> emplified the cultural ideal, the deviant stands for that to
> which the culture stands opposed. The group derives vitality
> from repulsion, indignation, and official reaction to deviant
> conduct. By calling attention to the sins, pathologies, and
> crimes of the outcast, the group reinforces its cohesiveness
> and reaffirms its norms. [1982: 28].

The visible responses to violations of normative standards serve to communicate to the young the limits that are imposed upon their behavior and, by implication, the behaviors that are required of them. Further, the collective response to the deviant behavior reinforces a feeling of collective solidarity among the members of the society that (particularly in modern society) is otherwise divided by diverse value systems. The collective response to violation of basic norms reinforces the sense of what commonality the society does possess.

It would follow from this that beliefs in the morality or immorality of certain acts may be influenced by the severity of reactions to those acts that the person perceives. The perceived severe reactions symbolize to the person the wrongness of the act. Tittle (1980), using survey data collected in three states, does in fact report relationships between perceived severity of sanctions associated with particular acts and judgments of the moral unacceptability of the acts. However, it cannot be determined whether the severity perceptions precede and influence judgment of morality and/or whether feelings about the morality of certain acts lead them to expect severe sanctions for violations of normative expectations. Tittle (1980: 74) points out: "If it could be shown that severity perceptions precede and lead to morality and seriousness judgments then a rational basis for maintaining or creating severe reactions would exist even if no direct deterrent effect operated." Tittle goes on to remind us that some social theorists have argued that the chief function of penalties is to reinforce and maintain the social order, rather than to deter deviance directly (Scott, 1971; Van den Haag, 1975).

The reactions to violations of the moral code, by influencing reaffirmation of the moral code, have implications for deterring the acting out of subsequent delinquent impulses. The social responses to violations of the moral code affirm the validity of the specific rules that are violated as well as the validity of the more inclusive moral code. With each punishment of a violation, the rule that is violated becomes more highly valued. As people more highly value the rule, they are less likely to become disposed to violate it. Thus, as Durkheim observed, within limits violation of the moral order serves a positive function for society by reaffirming and enhancing the value of the moral order. For this function to be served, the social response must clearly communicate through the administration of commensurately significant punishments the importance attached to the rule that was violated and, less directly, the importance of the moral order of which the rule is part. Conversely, it is to be expected by this reasoning that if the social response is of little significance to the audience, then the significance of the particular rule and, perhaps by implication, of the more inclusive moral order, will appear to be devalued. With devaluation of the prohibition, a person is more likely to become disposed to commit a delinquent act and is less likely to be deterred from acting out the deviant disposition. The resulting increased prevalence of the acts will further decrease condemnation of the acts in question.

SOCIAL CHANGE AND DELINQUENCY

While it may be true that occasional delinquency serves the function of reaffirming the values that the deviant behaviors deny, with increasing frequency, deviant behaviors serve to call into question the worth of these values, and deviant behaviors become stimuli for social change. If deviant behavior is viewed as evoking social responses that reinforce the validity of the social rules that are violated, then such behavior must also be viewed as having the potentially counteracting effect of laying the groundwork for social change in the moral code. Each instance of delinquent behavior is a potential stimulus and model for the acting out of preexisting deviant dispositions. Individuals who are disposed to violate rules may not yet have acted out their disposition because of the absence of a situational stimulus or because of the lack of a conception of what form the acting out might take. When the person who is so stimulated observes a delinquent act, he may be stimulated to act out his disposition to commit a delinquent act and, at the same time, may be provided with a delinquent model that provides the form that the acting-out of the deviant tendency might take. In short, one of the social consequences of delinquent behavior is the increased likelihood that others will act out the delinquent patterns.

Over time, the increased prevalence and visibility of the socially forbidden pattern mitigates the severity of the negative social attitudes and sanctions evoked by the pattern. What was once a forbidden pattern slowly becomes an acceptable one. Initial violations of a rule indirectly lead to a social change in the acceptability of the pattern.

How rapidly this process occurs is, in part, a function of the certainty and severity of punishments and other factors that have been observed to constrain the acting out of delinquent impulses. These factors, in turn, presume changing social attitudes. That is, the failure of the legal institutions to respond forcefully to particular violations at any given time indicates that the social attitudes toward the violation have changed. The rules are no longer regarded as sacred, the violations of the rule are no longer abhorrent, and the sanctions are no longer stringent and immediately administered. The attitudes toward the violation may not have changed in any absolute sense but rather only relative to other rules. Do changing attitudes toward capital punishment reflect an increasing acceptance of (a decreasing abhorrence of) capital crimes and/or an increased affirmation of human life regardless of its moral condition?

SUMMARY

Patterns of juvenile delinquency have consequences that reflect or influence the functioning of the social system and indirectly influence future performance of delinquency. A relatively direct outcome of delinquent patterns is the institutionalization of formal investigative, judicial, and correctional processes. Such responses, along with a number of less formal precautionary responses on the part of the public, are provoked in part by the attitudinal responses toward delinquency that are associated with more or less direct experience with victimization by the crimes. The nature of the response depends upon the characteristics of the offense, the offender, and the victim. The formal and informal responses may act as constraining influences that deter people from acting out delinquent impulses. However, it is possible that such responses may only redirect the delinquent impulse.

Delinquent behavior has a disruptive effect upon the social functioning of the delinquent, of those with whom the delinquent interacts, and of the victims. Moreover, the displacement of resources required to counteract the delinquent patterns preclude the achievement of other social goals that also require use of scarce resources, and, the responses provoked by the fear of delinquency frequently threaten other cherished values.

Yet, the negative sanctions applied to the offender that are provoked by the delinquent act serve to reinforce belief in the conventional morality and, thereby, to deter acting out of delinquent impulses.

As the same time that occasional delinquency serves the functions of reaffirming social values, such behavior lays the groundwork for effecting changes in the social acceptability of the behavior. Each instance of delinquent behavior is a potential stimulus and model for the acting out of delinquent dispositions.

DISCUSSION QUESTIONS

1. What evidence is there from different areas of life that attacks upon one's beliefs cause one to believe all the more strongly?

2. What examples can you describe of situations where increasing violations of norms lead to changing feelings about the behavior that violates the norms?

3. How does fear of delinquency in your situation affect your way of life? If juvenile delinquency was inconceivable, how would your life be changed?

8

TOWARD A GENERAL THEORY
OF JUVENILE DELINQUENCY

As we have seen, the explanation of the onset, continuity, and consequences of delinquent behavior is complex. The theoretical and empirical statements described in the first seven chapters present relationships in which (1) variables more or less directly affect each other, (2) variables affect other variables indirectly by first influencing mediating factors that in turn influence the other variables, (3) variables have counteracting effects in that the same variables through one set of influences lead to an increase in a variable and through another set of influences lead to a decrease in the same variable, (4), variables have particular kinds of effect only when certain circumstances are present but have no effects or opposite effects when such circumstances are not present.

The following brief summary of the content of the volume is offered as an initial and tentative formulation of the general relationships existing among variables that influence the onset, continuity of involvement in, and social consequences of juvenile delinquency. The explanation of juvenile delinquency is not to be found in one or even a few of these relationships but, rather, is reflected in the simultaneously considered web of such relationships.

SOCIAL DEFINITION
OF JUVENILE DELINQUENCY

The fact that certain behavior is socially defined as juvenile delinquency will stimulate or inhibit motivation to perform delinquent acts (and, therefore, the performance of delinquent acts) as well as change in level of involvement in delinquent activity. This depends upon a number of conditions. In general, the social definition of behavior as delinquent will stimulate motivation to perform delinquent acts where the youth is alienated from the conventional social structure and will inhibit motivation to perform delinquent acts where the youth is emotionally invested in conforming to conventional standards. The prevalence of delinquency that is partly the result of the social definition of behavior as delinquent, in turn, influences the social definition of the behavior as acceptable. The social definition of delinquent behavior influences the continuity of delinquent behavior through its effects on punitive patterns that under various conditions will induce motivation to conform to conventional standards or will increase physical and emotional distance between the offender and conventional society. As a result of the increased distance, the administration of negative sanctions by conventional society will be less effective.

The *causes* of social definitions of behavior as delinquent (through their effects on social definition) indirectly influence motivation to perform delinquent acts as well as the continuity of delinquency. Social definition of delinquency is influenced by the coexistence of culturally diverse groups at a given point in time, the rapid and uneven social change that creates cultural diversity over time, and the differential political influence exercised by particular segments of the population.

MOTIVATION TO COMMIT DELINQUENT ACTS
VIOLATING MEMBERSHIP GROUP NORMS

A youth is more likely to perform a delinquent act if he (consciously or unconsciously) anticipates that the delinquent act will result in satisfaction of salient needs. Certain of the youth's needs reflect the inability to meet the expectations of the conventional groups to which the youth belongs. The nature of the expectations and the feelings that the ability to meet those expectations is an appropriate measure of self-worth are learned in the course of the socialization process. The distressful feelings of self-rejection that accompany failure to meet the expectations of conventional groups (the use of conventional means to those ends being part of the expectations) motivates the youth to behave in deviant (including delinquent) ways that offer promise of gaining or restoring feelings of self-worth. The delinquent patterns may appear to the youth to have the likely consequences (1) of gaining legitimate goals through illegitimate means; (2) of avoiding or attacking the conventional standards by whose measure the youth judges himself to be worthless; (3) or of substituting new (delinquent) standards by which the youth might more favorably evaluate himself.

The inability to meet what the youth regards as justifiable expectations (including receiving positive responses from others for approximating the standards) reflects a lack of congruence between the demands made upon the youth (by self and others) and the available interpersonal, intrapsychic, or material resources to successfully meet those demands. The real or anticipated failure of the youth to meet personal and social expectations is a function of levels and kinds of social expectations being too high or the required resources being too few to successfully meet the demands made upon the youth. The levels of social expectations or personal aspirations and of available resources are defined by the role expectations that apply to the youth's various social identities (including those that indicate group affiliations). Therefore, the compatibility between demands and resources is influenced by the youth's various social identities, changes in normative life events that influence changes in the social identities and the roles that define them, and social changes in the role definition of particular social identities.

MOTIVATION TO COMMIT DELINQUENT ACTS CONFORMING TO MEMBERSHIP GROUP NORMS

Other of the youth's needs reflect the desire to receive approving responses from groups that endorse delinquent behaviors. Such approval is for the youth a measure of his self-worth. To the extent that approval of the group is earned by performing delinquent acts (or to the extent that the youth perceives the situation as such), the youth will be motivated to perform delinquent acts.

The groups that intrinsically value the delinquent acts or value them as reflections of more basic values may constitute groups in which the youth holds membership and was socialized or in which he aspires to hold membership. The groups that share delinquent norms (that is, endorse delinquent acts) may reflect a process whereby group members continue to conform to traditional standards that have come to be defined as illegal by more politically influential groups. Alternatively, the groups may reflect the end product of a process whereby members, who share the circumstances leading to failure to achieve according to the conventional standards in the course of social interaction, adopt delinquent patterns as collective solutions to their common need to gain or restore a sense of self-worth. Toward this end, they endorse the use of illicit activities that permit the achievement of conventional goals, attacks upon or withdrawal from the conventional standards that are the measure of their failure, or the substitution of different and more easily attainable standards as the measure of their self-worth.

The persistence of the delinquent subculture over successive groups depends upon the cultural transmissions of delinquency-endorsing standards to those who do not yet share the subculture, the rewarding of those who conform to the standards, and the punishing of those who deviate from the standards. The neophyte is either introduced into the group early and remains in the group over a long enough period of time to permit socialization into the delinquent subculture or later is attracted to the group as a source of gratification that stands in contrast to the conventional world from which the youth is alienated. In the latter case, the illegal nature of certain of the activities may be intrinsically gratifying (they are attractive because they are illegal) or merely may be the means to the end of being accepted by and of identifying with the group.

ACTING OUT DELINQUENT DISPOSITIONS

Whether or not a youth who is motivated to perform delinquent acts in fact performs such acts depends on the youth's experience of counteracting motives and opportunities to perform the acts. A youth is more likely to perform a delinquent act, which he or she is motivated to perform, if the youth does not feel that the performance would threaten the satisfaction of important needs or that nonperformance of the act would satisfy important needs. Conversely, a youth is less likely to perform a delinquent act that he or she is motivated to perform if the youth believes that the performance of the act would threaten the satisfaction of other important needs or that nonperformance of the act would satisfy important needs. Generally, the competing needs are derived from participation in the conventional socialization process in the course of which the youth learns that important needs are satisfied by conforming to expectations that are applicable to those who share his social identities, and that the satisfaction of salient needs is threatened by deviating from social identity-appropriate expectations.

The effective socialization of the youth in these terms, such that need-satisfaction is associated in the youth's mind with conformity and frustration of need satisfaction is associated with violation of identity-appropriate normative expectations, depends upon continuing association with conventional groups and some degree of success in achieving rewards associated with the approximation of conventionally valued standards. In the absence of continuing association with conventional groups, the youth will not learn what is expected of him, but, rather he will come to evaluate himself in terms of the nonconventional standards of the groups with which he does associate. In the absence of successful approximation of conventional standards, the youth, failing to receive needed rewards and, indeed, being punished for his failure to approximate conventional standards, will become alienated from the standards. Any factors that diminish the association of the youth with conventional groups or decrease the experience of need satisfactions in the context of conventional group processes will decrease the youth's emotional commitment to the rewards to be gained from conformity to and the punishments associated with deviation from conventional standards. Hence, to that extent, the youth who is motivated to engage in deviant activities will feel less inhibited from acting out the deviant dispositions.

In the presence of stable emotional commitment to the achievement of conventionally defined rewards and to the avoidance of conventionally defined punishments, any circumstances that impede the person's momentary awareness of the relationship between projected delinquent behavior and frustration of need-satisfaction will necessarily weaken the inhibition against acting out delinquent impulses. So, too, will the ability to justify the delinquent behavior in terms of conventional values.

Even in the absence of counteracting motives, the youth cannot perform the delinquent act he is motivated to perform without opportunities to do so. The more general the motive to violate conventional norms, the greater the range of delinquent acts that may satisfy the need, and, as the range of appropriate delinquent impulses increase, so do the opportunities to perform one or another of the delinquent responses.

The awareness of opportunities to perform delinquent activities decreases as the youth's involvement in conventional activities increases and as opportunities for more favorable conventional approaches to problem resolution become available. However, at the same time, involvement in conventional roles influences the form that delinquent responses take (in the absence of more favorable response patterns) since many delinquent responses are illicit extensions of conventional response dispositions learned in the course of the socialization process.

The opportunities for delinquent behavior are increased by circumstances influencing the existence of stable delinquent subcultures in the environment and favorable interaction with those who share the subculture. Such opportunities are decreased by effective negative sanctions for delinquent behavior that diminish the availability of delinquent role models as well as the means and occasions for delinquent activities.

CONTINUITY OF DELINQUENT BEHAVIOR

Delinquent behavior will continue to be repeated or increase if the youth perceives a relationship between the satisfaction of his needs and the delinquent behavior, if the motives that ordinarily inhibit the performance of delinquent acts are weakened, and if the opportunities to perform delinquent behavior remain apparent or are perceived as increasingly available. Positive reinforcement of delinquent patterns will be achieved if the youth experiences satisfaction of his needs and attributes satisfaction of the needs to the delinquent activities. The need-satisfaction might be accomplished through the illicit achievement of conventional values, avoidance of or attacks upon the conventional standards that are the measure of the youth's failure, the substitution of deviant standards by the measure of which the youth may more easily judge himself to be worthy, gaining the approval of a positive reference group that endorses delinquent activities, or the validation of earlier delinquent behavior or of the deviant identity that is the consequence of the earlier delinquent behavior.

Weakening of social controls (counteracting motives) is the consequence of failure to observe visible adverse consequences of delinquent behavior and of the decreased attraction to conventional groups resulting from the continuation of processes that induced the initial delinquent dispositions and the rejecting responses of conventional groups to the youth's initial delinquent acts. These rejecting responses and the associated alienation from the conventional groups increase the youth's attraction to and association with delinquent groups that provide both the occasions and opportunities for delinquent behavior.

The decrease in or discontinuation of delinquent behavior is likely to occur to the extent that (1) the delinquent patterns do not appear to satisfy the needs that stimulated the delinquent responses, (2) the delinquent behaviors stimulate threats to the satisfaction of other needs such as those associated with the desire for continuing involvement with conventional morality or with fear of formal sanctions, and (3) changes in the youth's needs or in the availability of conventional opportunities render delinquent behavior unnecessary.

CONSEQUENCES OF DELINQUENCY

Patterns of delinquency provoke mutually influential consequences that, in turn, influence subsequent delinquent behavior. Delinquent patterns provoke public attitudinal responses and associated formal (investigative, judicial, correctional) and informal (social rejection, precautionary tactics) behavioral responses. The nature of the response is a function of the characteristics of the offense, offender, and victim. These responses under different conditions constrain the acting out of delinquent impulses, increase the fixity of the early offender in a delinquent career, and displace the deviant impulses on to alternate targets.

Delinquent patterns have more direct effects upon the social functioning of the delinquent and his victim, as well as of those in his social sphere and, less directly, upon the ability to achieve social values. The attainment of these values depends upon the scarce resources diverted to the containment of delinquency and upon the extent to which the nature and consequences of the responses provoked by delinquency reflect or violate social values.

More positively, the violation of collective standards provoke responses that reaffirm the collective sentiment in favor of the moral code that was violated. The reaffirmation of the moral code functions to deter delinquent impulses. Counterbalancing this tendency, however, is the groundwork for change in the social definition of the acceptability of the delinquent behaviors. Visible violations of the code, depending upon the social responses evoked and the degree of alienation of the population from the conventional order, may stimulate and provide models for delinquent patterns among invididuals who are disposed to so behave. With increasing prevalence, the delinquent act appears to be more acceptable, thus further weakening the deterrent effect of social attitudes and associated behavioral responses toward delinquency.

CONCLUSION

The purpose of this volume was not to provide a final explanation of the onset, continuity, and consequences of juvenile delinquency. Rather, the purpose was to describe ongoing theoretical developments and reseach findings that reflect the complexity of the explanation. At the same time, the summary of these developments serves as a framework for the integration of new research findings and reformulated theoretical positions based on these findings toward the goal of providing a comprehensive explanation of juvenile delinquency as a sociological phenomenon. Once again, such a comprehensive explanation is to be found, not in one or in a few of the relationships reviewed above, but rather is to be found in the web of simultaneously considered relationships that concern the onset, continuity, and consequences of juvenile delinquency.

REFERENCES

BEAN, F. D. and R. G. CUSHING (1971) "Criminal homicide, punishment, and deterrence: Methodological and substantive reconsiderations." Social Science Quarterly 52: 277-289.

BECKER, H. S. (1963) Outsiders: Studies in the Sociology of Deviance. New York: Free Press.

BERK, R. A., K. J. LENIHAN, and P. H. ROSSI (1980) "Crime and poverty: Some experimental evidence from ex-offenders." American Sociological Review 45: 766-786.

BRIAR, S. and I. PILIAVIN (1965) "Delinquency, situational inducements, and commitment to conformity." Social Problems 13: 35-45.

CHEIN, I. (1966) "Psychological, social and epidemiological factors in drug addiction," pp. 53-72 in Rehabilitating the Narcotic Addict. Fort Worth, TX: Institute on New Developments in the Rehabilitation of the Narcotic Addict.

CLARK, J. P. and E. P. WENNINGER (1962) "Socioeconomic class and areas as correlates of illegal behavior among juveniles." American Sociological Review 27: 826-834.

CLOWARD, R. A. and L. E. OHLIN (1960) Delinquency and Opportunity. New York: Free Press.

COHEN, A. K. (1955) Delinquent Boys. Glencoe, IL: Free Press.

CONGER, R. D. (1976) "Social control and social learning models of delinquent behavior: A synthesis." Criminology 14: 17-40.

DURKHEIM, E. (1938) The Rules of Sociological Method (S. A. Solovay and J. H. Mueller, trans.; G.E.G. Catlin, ed.). New York: Macmillan.

ELLIOTT, D. S. (1961) "Delinquency, opportunity, and patterns of orientations." Doctoral dissertation, University of Washington, Seattle.

———(1966) "Delinquency, school attendance and dropout." Social Problems 13: 307-314.

———and H. L. VOSS (1974) Delinquency and Dropout. Lexington, MA: D. C. Heath.

FARRELL, R. A. and V. L. SWIGERT (1982) Deviance and Social Control. Glenview, IL: Scott, Foresman.

FELDMAN, H. W. (1968) "Ideological supports to becoming and remaining a heroin addict." Journal of Health and Social Behavior 9: 131-139.

FURSTENBERG, F. F., Jr. (1971) "Public reactions to crime in the streets." American Scholar 40: 601-610.

GERSTEN, J. C., T. S. LANGER, J. G. EISENBERG, O. SIMCHA-FAGAN, and E. D. McCARTHY (1976) "Stability and change in types of behavioral disturbance of children and adolescents." Journal of Abnormal Child Psychology 4: 111-127.

GIBBONS, D. C. (1976) Delinquent Behavior. Englewood Cliffs, NJ: Prentice-Hall.

GIBBS, J. P. (1968) "Crime, punishment, and deterrence." Social Science Quarterly 48: 515-530.

HEPBURN, J. R. (1976) "Testing alternative models of delinquency causation." Journal of Criminal Law and Criminology 67: 450-460.

HEWITT, J. P. (1970) Social Stratification and Deviant Behavior. New York: Random House.

HINDELANG, M. J. (1973) "Causes of delinquency: A partial replication and extension." Social Problems 20: 471-487.

———(1974) "Moral evaluations and illegal behaviors." Social Problems 21: 370-385.

———T. HIRSCHI, and J. G. WEIS (1981) Measuring Delinquency. Beverly Hills, CA: Sage.

HIRSCHI, T. (1969) Causes of Delinquency. Berkeley: University of California Press.

JOHNSON, R. E. (1979) Juvenile Delinquency and Its Origins. New York: Cambridge University Press.

KAPLAN, H. B. (1972) "Toward a general theory of psychosocial deviance: The case of aggressive behavior." Social Science and Medicine 6: 593-617.

———(1975) Self-Attitudes and Deviant Behavior. Santa Monica, CA: Goodyear.

———(1980) Deviant Behavior in Defense of Self. New York: Academic Press.

———(1982) "Self-attitudes and deviant behavior: New directions for theory and research." Youth and Society 14: 185-211.

———S. S. MARTIN, and C. ROBBINS (1982) "Application of a general theory of deviant behavior: Self-derogation and adolescent drug use." Journal of Health and Social Behavior 23: 274-294.

KAPLAN, H. B. and C. ROBBINS (1983) "Testing a general theory of deviant behavior in longitudinal perspective," pp. 117-146 in K. Van Dusen and S. A. Mednick (eds.), Prospective Studies in Delinquent and Criminal Behavior. Boston, MA: Kluwer-Nijhoff.

———and S. S. MARTIN (1984) "Subcultural variation in multivariate models of self-attitudes and delinquent behavior," pp. 73-108 in J. R. Greenley (ed.), Research in Community and Mental Health, vol. 4. Greenwich, CT: JAI Press.

KOBRIN, S. (1951) "The conflict of values in delinquency areas." American Sociological Review 16: 653-661.

LIND, A. W. (1938) Island Community: A Study of Ecological Successions in Hawaii. Chicago: University of Chicago Press.

MATZA, D. (1964) Delinquency and Drift. New York: John Wiley.

MERTON, R. K. (1957) Social Theory and Social Structure. New York: Free Press.

MILLER, W. B. (1958) "Lower class culture as a generating milieu of gang delinquency." Journal of Social Issues 14: 5-19.

NYE, F. I. (1958) Family Relationships and Delinquent Behavior. New York: John Wiley.

ODELL, B. N. (1974) "Accelerating entry into the opportunity structure: A sociologically based treatment for delinquent youth." Sociology and Social Research 58: 312-317.

PALMER, J. (1977) "Economic analysis of the deterrent effect of punishment: A review." Journal of Research in Crime and Delinquency 14: 4-21.

POLK, K. and D. HALFERTY (1966) "Adolescence, commitment, and delinquency." Journal of Research in Crime and Delinquency 4: 82-96.

RECKLESS, W. C., S. DINITZ, and E. MURRAY (1956) "Self-concept as an insulator against delinquency." American Sociological Review 21: 744-746.

ROFF, M. (1977) "Long-term follow-up of juvenile and adult delinquency with samples differing in some important respects: Cross-validation within the same research program," pp. 75-116 in J. S. Strauss, H. M. Babigian, and M. Roff (eds.), The Origins and Course of Psychopathology. New York: Plenum.

SCOTT, J. F. (1971) Internalization of Norms: A Sociological Theory of Moral Commitment. Englewood Cliffs, NJ: Prentice-Hall.

SELLIN, T. (1938) Culture Conflict and Crime. New York: Social Science Research Council, Bulletin 41.

SHAW, C. and H. D. McKAY (1942) Juvenile Delinquency in Urban Areas. Chicago: University of Chicago Press.

SIEGAL, L. J., S. A. RATHUS, and C. A. RUPPERT (1973) "Values and delinquency." British Journal of Criminology 13: 237-244.

SKOGAN, W. G. and M. G. MAXFIELD (1981) Coping with Crime: Individual and Neighborhood Reactions. Beverly Hills, CA: Sage.

SUTHERLAND, E. H. (1937) The Professional Thief. Chicago: University of Chicago Press.

SYKES, G. M. and D. MATZA (1957) "Techniques of neutralization: A theory of delinquency." American Sociological Review 22: 664-670.

TITTLE, C. R. (1980) Sanctions and Social Deviance: The Question of Deterrence. New York: Praeger.

VAN den HAAG, E. (1975) Punishing Criminals: Concerning a Very Old and Painful Question. New York: Basic Books.

WIATROWSKI, M. D., D. B. GRISWOLD, and M. K. ROBERTS (1981) "Social control theory and delinquency." American Sociological Review 46: 525-541.

WINICK, C. (1964) "The life cycle of the narcotic addict and of addiction." Bulletin on Narcotics 16: 1-11.

———(1980) "A theory of drug dependence based on role, access to, and attitudes toward drugs," pp. 225-235 in D. J. Lettieri, M. Sayers, and H. W. Pearson (eds.), Theories on Drug Abuse: Selected Contemporary Perspectives. Rockville, MD: National Institute on Drug Abuse.

———and J. GOLDSTEIN (1965) The Glue Sniffing Problem. New York: American Social Health Association.

ZIMRING, F. E. and G. HAWKINS (1973) Deterrence: The Legal Threat in Crime Control. Chicago: University of Chicago Press.